Mobilizing Resources, Building Coalitions:
Local Power in Indonesia

Policy Studies

an East-West Center series

Series Editors: Edward Aspinall and Dieter Ernst

Description

Policy Studies presents scholarly analysis of key contemporary domestic and international political, economic, and strategic issues affecting Asia in a policy relevant manner. Written for the policy community, academics, journalists, and the informed public, the peer-reviewed publications in this series provide new policy insights and perspectives based on extensive fieldwork and rigorous scholarship.

The East-West Center is pleased to announce that the Policy Studies series has been accepted for indexing in the Web of Science Book Citation Index. The Web of Science is the largest and most comprehensive citation index available. The quality and depth of content Web of Science offers to researchers, authors, publishers, and institutions sets it apart from other research databases. The inclusion of Policy Studies in the Book Citation Index demonstrates our dedication to providing the most relevant and influential content to our community.

Notes to Contributors

Submissions may take the form of a proposal or complete manuscript. For more information on the Policy Studies series, please contact the Series Editors.

Editors, *Policy Studies*
East-West Center
1601 East-West Road
Honolulu, Hawai'i 96848-1601
Tel: 808.944.7197
Publications@EastWestCenter.org
EastWestCenter.org/PolicyStudies

Policy Studies 64

Mobilizing Resources, Building Coalitions:
Local Power in Indonesia

Ryan Tans

Copyright © 2012 by the East-West Center

Mobilizing Resources, Building Coalitions: Local Power in Indonesia
Ryan Tans

ISSN 1547-1349 (print) and 1547-1330 (electronic)
ISBN 978-0-86638-235-9 (print) and 978-0-86638-236-6 (electronic)

Hard copies of all titles, and free electronic copies of most titles, are
available from:

Publication Sales Office
East-West Center
1601 East-West Road
Honolulu, Hawai'i 96848-1601
Tel: 808.944.7145
Fax: 808.944.7376
EWCBooks@EastWestCenter.org
EastWestCenter.org/PolicyStudies

In Asia, hard copies of all titles, and electronic copies of select Southeast Asia titles, co-published in Singapore, are available from:

Institute of Southeast Asian Studies
30 Heng Mui Keng Terrace
Pasir Panjang Road, Singapore 119614
publish@iseas.edu.sg
bookshop.iseas.edu.sg

Contents

List of Key Indonesian Terms and Acronyms

Bitra Indonesia	Bina Keterampilan Pedesaan Indonesia, Building Rural Skills in Indonesia (an NGO)
bupati	District Head (executive of a district)
Partai Demokrat	Democrat Party
DPR	Dewan Perwakilan Rakyat, National People's Representative Assembly
DPRD	Dewan Perwakilan Rakyat Daerah, Provincial, District, or Municipal People's Representative Assembly
Golkar	Golongan Karya (abbreviated Golkar), Functional Group (political party)
IPK	Ikatan Pemuda Karya, Functional Youth League
Kejaksaan	Office of the public prosecutor
KPK	Komisi Pemberantasan Korupsi, Anti-corruption Commission
MPI	Masyarakat Pancasila Indonesia, Community for Indonesian National Principles (youth organization)

PDI-P — Partai Demokrasi Indonesia—Perjuangan, Indonesian Democratic Party of Struggle

Pemuda Pancasila — Pancasila Youth

PKK — Pemberdayaan Kesejahteraan Keluarga, Family Welfare and Empowerment (a network of women's associations)

Pujakesuma — Putra Jawa Kelahiran Sumatera, Sons of Java Born in Sumatra

PPP — Partai Persatuan Pembangunan, United Development Party (Islamic orientation)

PKS — Partai Keadilan Sejahtera, Welfare and Justice Party (Islamic)

walikota — Mayor (executive of a municipality)

Executive Summary

What have been the local political consequences of Indonesia's de-centralization and electoral reforms? This question has attracted a great deal of scholarly and journalistic interest since 1999 because of its substantive importance. Local governments make decisions that impact, among others, village development programs, regional economies, national party politics, and the effectiveness of the well-publicized reforms.

Some recent scholarship on local politics has emphasized continuity with Suharto's New Order. This work has argued that under the new rules, old elites have used money and intimidation to capture elected office. Many of these studies have detailed the widespread practice of "money politics," in which candidates exchange patronage for support from voters and parties. Yet this work also acknowledges that significant variation characterizes Indonesia's local politics, suggesting the need for an approach that differentiates contrasting power arrangements.

This study of three districts in North Sumatra province compares local politicians according to their institutional resource bases and coalitional strategies. Even if all practice money politics, they form different types of coalitions that depend on diverse institutions for political resources. The most consequential institutions are bureaucracies, parties, legislatures, businesses, and social organizations. These provide different types and measures of resources—remunerative, symbolic, and sometimes coercive—that politicians put to work building coalitions and contesting power. By shifting analytical focus from money politics (which are all-too-common) to resource bases (which vary), this study produces a framework for characterizing local power.

The approach identifies three ideal types of coalitions: political mafias, party machines, and mobilizing coalitions. Political mafias have a resource base limited to local state institutions and businesses, party machines bridge local and supra-local institutions, and mobilizing coalitions incorporate social organizations and groups of voters. As a result of their varying composition, political competition among these coalitions occurs vertically. Machines, directed from the center, are oriented vertically upward; political mafias horizontally encompass local elites; and mobilizing coalitions, which cater to popular pressures, are oriented vertically downward.

The coalitions have different "menus" of strategic options due to their resource bases, raising the possibility that they may not always adopt the same political tactics. Machine politicians, who have the benefit of party influence within the provincial and central levels of government, enjoy two advantages over strictly local mafia politicians in terms of resources. First, they are likely to have more patronage at their disposal, and second, they have an enhanced ability to hinder their opponents through bureaucratic and electoral vetting procedures, district partitioning, and, in some cases, legal action. When faced with the prospect of losing power, both political mafias and party machines may attempt to gain an electoral advantage by constructing mobilizing coalitions. With more patronage at their disposal, machines are in a better position to spread it more widely within the district. As it reaches more people, patronage may start to resemble a public good with widespread benefits. To the extent that electoral competition compels mafias and machines to construct mobilizing coalitions, to provide public goods and to appeal to mass audiences, the potential exists for the emergence of a new kind of politics more closely resembling electoral pluralism than money politics.

This monograph presents detailed case studies that highlight the contests between elite coalitions in three districts in North Sumatra. In Labuhan Batu district, an opposition mafia used a strategy of mobilization to defeat an incumbent mafia. In Tapanuli Selatan district, the Golkar party machine displaced a timber mafia by subdividing the district into three new districts. Finally, in Serdang Bedagai district, all three types of coalitions have contended for power. In 2005, a local mafia gave way to the Golkar machine after the election resulted in a virtual tie. Once in office, Golkar pursued a strategy of mobilization and constructed a broad and reliable electoral coalition.

The three districts studied here were chosen because they vary economically and socially in ways similar to other Indonesian districts, especially in the Outer Islands. This variation, combined with their typical administrative institutions, means that it is plausible that other districts experience similar local politics. Closely observing the processes connecting political resources, electoral strategies and local regimes in the three districts lends confidence to the conclusion that corresponding coalitions may emerge in places where similar institutional resource bases are available to aspiring elites.

Across the province of North Sumatra in 2010, local elections were competitive and turnover was high. The competition between political mafias and party machines increased democratic participation in two ways. First, elections presented a meaningful choice to voters, as the difference in orientation between mafias and machines affected the local government's capacity to distribute patronage as well as its attitude toward important local issues such as plantation revenue sharing and forest reclassification. Second, close competition pressured some contending candidates to reach out to new constituencies in an effort to build mobilizing coalitions. Mafias and machines in some places incorporated NGOs, youth groups, farmers' associations, local communities, and religious associations. By involving their constituencies in the political process, these social organizations may, through the threat of withdrawing their support, help to hold local governments accountable.

However, recent national policy rolling back decentralization has weakened the political strength of mafias. Golkar's party machine won in several strategic jurisdictions in North Sumatra, including the capital city of Medan, while mafias fared poorly. In the future, more inclusive politics may decline if party machines stifle local electoral competition in the absence of assertive mafias.

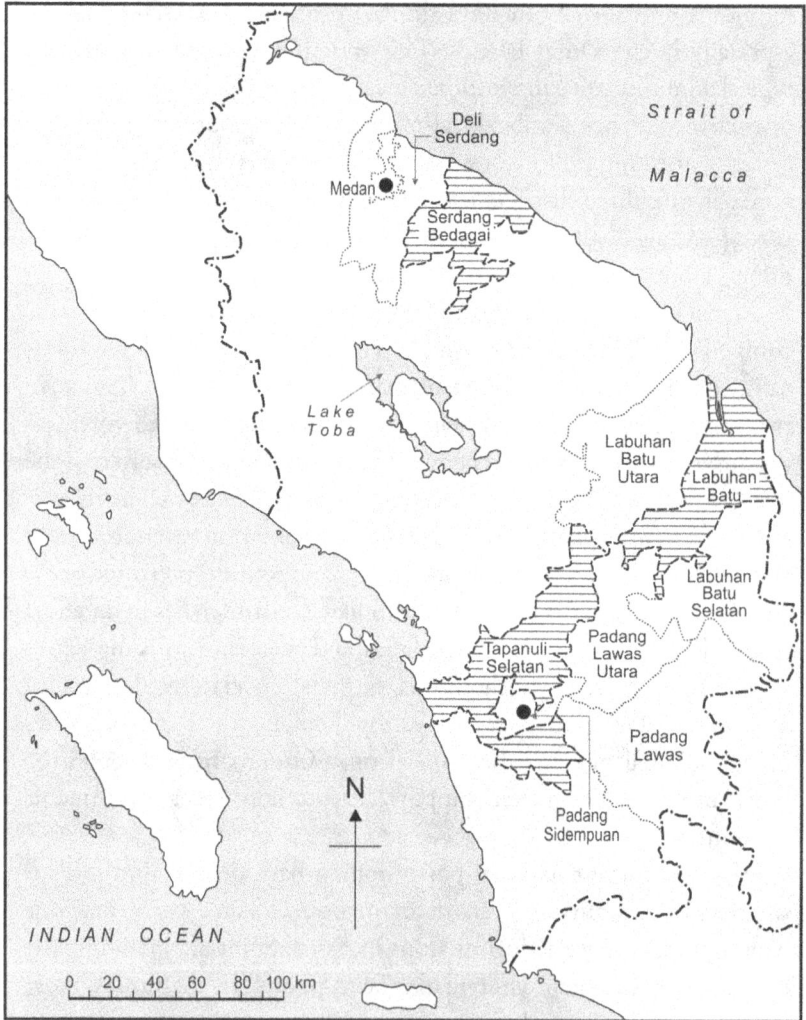

Map of North Sumatra Province

Mobilizing Resources, Building Coalitions:
Local Power in Indonesia

Introduction

In 2010, Indonesia entered its third round of local elections since the end of authoritarian rule in 1998 and the passage of decentralization reforms in 1999. Among other powers, the reforms gave district and municipal assemblies (Dewan Perwakilan Rakyat Daerah, DPRD) the authority to draft legislation, enact local taxes, and deliberate the administrative budget and gave district and municipal heads (*bupati* and *walikota*) the right to appoint bureaucrats and license some natural resource concessions.[1] In addition, the

Electoral reform encouraged thousands of candidates across Indonesia to compete for local office

reforms guaranteed local government revenues by providing that the central government would annually release block grants to each district and province.[2] Local government, comprising an assembly and an executive, assumed discretionary authority far beyond what it had possessed during Suharto's New Order regime.

Parallel electoral reform encouraged thousands of candidates across Indonesia to compete for local office. The first round of elections from

1999–2005 was indirect, in that popularly elected district assemblies voted to select executives.[3] Beginning with the second round in 2005, direct popular elections were held for the position of district heads. These contests have been intensely competitive. Some districts and cities have fielded more than ten candidates for the office despite the high cost of campaigning. Vote-buying and paying bribes to obtain party nominations have been commonplace. In rare instances, violence, especially against property, has marred the process (ICG 2010).

At the same time that the reforms were being instituted, the number of Indonesian districts and provinces proliferated because old administrative units were subdivided to create new, smaller ones.[4] From 1998 to 2004, the total number of districts increased from 292 to 434. More recently, district partitioning has continued but at a slower rate, so that in 2010 there were 491 Indonesian districts. These territorial changes further decentralized Indonesian politics by creating hundreds of new elected offices and branches of bureaucratic agencies at the local level (Kimura 2010).

New districts, competitive elections, and the discretionary powers of local government have generated a great deal of scholarly and journalistic interest in Indonesia's local politics. Local government decisions impact village development programs, local economies, national party politics, and the effectiveness of Indonesia's well-publicized reforms. Understanding these substantively important consequences of local politics requires knowledge about how local politicians achieve power through elections and how they exercise it while in office. To that end, this study investigates the coalitional and institutional sources of local power in post-reform Indonesia.

Characterizing Local Power

Most candidates for the position of district head previously pursued careers in business, the bureaucracy, party service, or parastatal youth organizations. In a survey of 50 local elections in 2005, Marcus Mietzner (2006) found that almost two-thirds of candidates were bureaucrats or entrepreneurs, and that another twenty-two percent were party officials. Vedi Hadiz (2010, 92–93) affirms a similar "political sociology of local elites," noting that local politics have been dominated by bureaucrats, entrepreneurs, and "goons and thugs" associated with the New Order's corporatist youth organizations. Notably absent are military officers, who in post-reform Indonesia have rarely won local office. Mietzner (2009a, 141) calls these politicians members of "the oligarchic elite," and Hadiz (2010, 3) argues that they "have been able to usurp…reforms…to sustain their social and political dominance." They are so well established, according to Michael Buehler (2010, 276), that "the majority of candidates competing in local elections… [are] closely affiliated with New Order networks," and even when incumbents lose elections they "have largely been replaced by representatives of the same old elite."

Some of these figures have been compared to "bosses" in the Philippines or criminal "godfathers" (*chao pho*) in Thailand (Sidel 1999, Ockey 2000). Hadiz (2010, 3–4) calls the arrangements "'local strongmen', corrupt local machineries of power… [and] pockets of authoritarianism." Henk Schulte Nordholt (2003, 579) refers to "regional shadow regimes," and John Sidel (2004, 69) describes "local 'mafias,' 'networks,' and 'clans,'" which are "loosely defined, somewhat shadowy, and rather fluid clusters and cliques of businessman, politicians, and officials."

Shadowy mafias may be common, but they are not ubiquitous. Recent scholarship has also identified other types of networks that contest local power. Buehler (2009, 102), for example, argues that "strong personal networks at the sub-district level" were necessary to win district office in South Sulawesi. Claire Smith, meanwhile, has argued that Golkar (Golongan Karya [Functional Group]), which had been the regime's electoral vehicle during the New Order, operated a party machine in North Maluku, notwithstanding the prevailing view that the local influence of political parties is in decline (Smith 2009; Tomsa 2009).

Meanwhile, the literature on ethnic and religious politics has highlighted the influence of elites who were excluded from power during the New Order. Since the regime collapsed, cultural elites have played pivotal roles—both destructive and constructive—in local politics. In some districts, violent militias and riotous mobs mobilized around ethnic and religious identities, while in others, ethnic and religious traditions have mediated popular organizing and widespread political participation (Davidson 2009; Davidson and Henley 2007). Old aristocracies and royal houses, traditional symbols of ethnic leadership, have reemerged as well and attempted to convert their symbolic power into political influence.

The literature demonstrates wide variation among politically influential local elites. "New Order elites" are not monolithic: they include politicians, businessmen, bureaucrats, and thugs. Grassroots networks matter in some districts, while parties play different roles across the country. Cultural elites mobilize their followers to participate in diverse forms of collective action. Any analysis of local politics after Indonesia's decentralization reforms must account for such variation.

What is the best way to characterize systematically local political variation? This study proposes that the concept of clientelism, carefully applied, can provide a basis for comparison. This approach builds on Gerry van Klinken (2009, 144), who refers to "patronage democracy" in which local elites "derive their power mainly from the state, and...relate with their constituency through clientelistic practices." The "money politics" of clientelism, that is, the reciprocal exchange of material goods and promises of patronage for support, have been carefully described (Hidayat 2009). This study adds an examination of institutional resource bases and the political coalitions they support in order to distinguish variation within the practice of clientelism. Since money politics are practiced within a variety of regimes, studies that emphasize them to the detriment of other dimensions of clientelism may not observe differences across districts or among individuals when patronage is the norm, potentially creating the appearance of an undifferentiated political elite.

This study argues that at least three types of coalitions contend for district-level political power in Indonesia. Each coalition is associated with a particular set of institutions that provide it with a resource base. *Mafias* control local state institutions. *Machines* are organized around the backing of a major political party. *Mobilizing coalitions* seek to mobilize and incorporate previously excluded social constituencies. Mobilization as a strategy is available to both mafias and machines, but in pursuing it mafias and machines may be transformed into a distinct third type of coalition. As mobilizing coalitions, they must accommodate the collective expectations of new groups that are neither part of the state nor the constituents of political parties. These different types of coalitions have contrasting sets of strategic options that are based on the resources available to their associated institutions. Finally, political contention among these types of coalitions is oriented vertically. Machines, oriented vertically upward, are directed from the center; political mafias, oriented horizontally, encompass local elites; and mobilizing coalitions, oriented vertically downward, cater to popular pressures.

Case Selection and Methodology
This study develops the framework through detailed case studies in three districts in North Sumatra province: Labuhan Batu, Tapanuli Selatan, and Serdang Bedagai. These districts are similar in that they operate within the same national and provincial institutions, but they experienced different outcomes. Over two elections, in 2005 and 2010, each district experienced competition among mafias, machines, and mobilizing coalitions,

At least three types of coalitions contend for district-level political power in Indonesia: mafias, machines, and mobilizing coalitions

but different coalitions prevailed. In Labuhan Batu, a mobilizing coalition succeeded a political mafia; in Tapanuli Selatan, a party machine succeeded a mafia; and in Serdang Bedagai, a mobilizing coalition succeeded a machine that had succeeded a mafia.

The three districts studied here were chosen because they vary economically and socially in ways similar to other Indonesian districts, especially in the Outer Islands. This variation, combined with their typical administrative institutions, means that it is plausible that other districts experience similar local politics. Economically, two of the three districts depend on agricultural products and natural resources, while the third district has a diversified economy that features agricultural products. Socially, the cases vary from rural, poor, and remote Tapanuli Selatan to an urban hinterland in Serdang Bedagai.

Institutionally, district governments in North Sumatra are subject to the same fiscal, electoral, and bureaucratic arrangements as the rest of Indonesia, albeit with important exceptions. Fiscally, they operate with much smaller budgets than the most densely populated districts on Java and districts that receive substantial revenue-sharing payments (such as in parts of East Kalimantan, Riau, South Sulawesi, and Papua). Nor should they be compared to districts in Indonesia's five special autonomous regions (Aceh, Jakarta, Yogyakarta, Papua, and West Papua), which are governed by special fiscal and electoral laws.

The conclusions of this study are based on a comparison of the resource bases and strategies of mafias, machines, and mobilizing coalitions—both successful and unsuccessful—in the three districts. By selecting cases that exhibit as much variation in outcomes as possible, the study avoids the problem of selection bias that occurs in a "truncated sample" of cases with similar outcomes (Collier and Mahoney 1996, 61). Further, closely observing the processes connecting political resources, electoral strategies, and local regimes lends confidence to the conclusion that similar patterns may occur in other districts where similar institutional resource bases are available to aspiring elites (Kuhonta et al. 2008, 7). However, it is possible that the cases do not capture the full range of variation that occurs in Indonesia such that other types of coalitions may be found elsewhere.

The case studies draw on 78 unstructured interviews conducted in North Sumatra in 2010. The interview sources include journalists, politicians, civil servants, election commissioners, businessmen, and NGO activists. Their names are withheld for confidentiality. Archival newspaper research augments the interviews. As much as possible, newspaper sources were consulted for the years 2005–2010 in order to cover two elections. Press statements released by NGOs in North Sumatra are a valuable source of additional data, as too are government publications, especially the Central Statistics Bureau's Statistical Yearbooks and election data published by election commissions.

> *The case studies are based on 78 interviews with journalists, politicians, civil servants, election commissioners, businessmen, and NGO activitsts*

Mobilizing Resources, Building Coalitions

Elites exercise power to the degree that their influence over institutions allows them to deliver resources. Charles Tilly (1978) developed a model for collective action in which contending groups mobilize resources as they struggle for power. Dan Slater classifies those resources as coercive, remunerative, and symbolic, noting that different sets of elites have access to different resources in varying proportion (Slater 2010, 16). The value of the resources at the disposal of a particular organization depends on its relationship to other contending groups. For example, Martin Shefter (1994, 61–63) explains in the context of the American party system that when parties are strong and the bureaucracy is weak, parties may override the bureaucracy to extract resources from the state for the construction of patronage machines.

In Indonesia, elites rely on what James Scott (1972, 97–98) once called a "resource base of patronage" composed mainly of "indirect, office-based property." However, different offices provide different resources, and elites can expand their resource base by forming coalitions across multiple offices or organizations. Some politicians reach beyond the district to acquire resources from provincial or national levels of government. Accordingly, this study distinguishes between political mafias, which mobilize resources exclusively at the local level, and party machines, which combine local and supra-local resources.

Political parties enable politicians to bridge local, provincial, and national levels of government. Not all parties are capable of this, however. Parties must have sufficient influence to expropriate provincial resources for partisan purposes. The best way to obtain such influence is by controlling the governor's mansion, but perhaps parties can achieve similar ends through legislative or bureaucratic influence.

Party machines are more likely than political mafias to be successful in their efforts to construct mobilizing coalitions because they have larger resource bases. However, due to the expense of attracting new constituents they are not necessarily more likely to attempt to do so. Politicians who have the benefit of party influence within the provincial and central levels of government enjoy two advantages over strictly local politicians in terms of resources. First, they are likely to have more patronage at their disposal, and second, they have an enhanced ability to hinder their opponents through bureaucratic and electoral vetting procedures, district partitioning, and, in some cases, legal action. These advantages give them a longer "menu" of strategic options, raising the possibility that they may experiment with different voter mobilization tactics than their local rivals. With more patronage at their disposal, machines are in a better position to spread it more widely within the district. As patronage reaches more people, it may start to resemble a public good with widespread benefits. Further, in closely contested elections, machines should have better capacity to experiment with alternatives to patronage, either by undermining their opponents or by playing mass politics. To the extent that electoral competition compels mobilizing coalitions to provide public goods and appeal to mass audiences, the potential exists for the emergence of a new kind of politics more closely resembling electoral pluralism than clientelism.

The next section outlines the pressures encouraging the formation of coalitions, while the following section describes the institutions associated with each type of coalition and the resources and strategies that flow from them.

Coalitions, Not Strongmen

There is a widespread misperception among political observers of Indonesia that decentralization has liberated district heads from vertical oversight and horizontal accountability. According to the Indonesian press, district heads adopt the style of "little kings." In the words of the *Economist* (2011), "Prospective candidates rack up big debts to bribe voters and political parties. Then, they resort to embezzlement in office to pay the debts." In this way they circumvent electoral accountability. However, the debts with which district heads take office and the risks they bear of corruption prosecution are evidence of other accountability mechanisms at work.

> *There is a widespread misperception that decentralization has liberated district heads from vertical oversight and horizontal accountability*

Debts oblige executives to answer to creditors and are part and parcel of horizontal checks that exist at the local level. In addition, the central government has the authority to exercise vertical oversight in a variety of ways, including prosecuting corruption, disbursing local revenues, auditing local expenditures, and overturning local legislation. Although it is convenient to reduce local government to the actions of district heads, in fact their behavior is highly circumscribed.

Local elections are expensive. Estimates range from US$500,000–700,000 in "resource-poor districts" to US$1.6 million (Buehler 2009, fn. 20; Sukardi 2005). By contrast, district budgets are limited and district heads do not enjoy full discretionary authority over them. In the average 2010 budget, 61 percent of annual expenditures covered fixed administrative costs, leaving Rp 260 billion (US$29 million) available for discretionary procurement and development spending (DPK 2010). A district head who depends on budget fraud to raise political funds will attempt to capture these funds by marking up the value of tendered projects and by demanding kickbacks from successful contractors.

To achieve this, a district head needs the cooperation of local business contractors, high-level bureaucrats, and district assembly members (van Klinken and Aspinall 2011). Business contractors must agree to the terms and pay the kickbacks. The bureaucrats directing government agencies must collaborate because they manage the projects. The assembly must acquiesce because it passes the annual budget (Anggaran Pendapatan dan Belanjaan Daerah, APBD) and budget report (*Pertanggungjawaban Pelaksanaan* APBD), and debates the annual executive performance review. Although Buehler notes that assemblies' oversight powers have diminished since Law No. 32/2004, they nevertheless can still frustrate the executive during these deliberations. As a result, district heads continue to "buy off parliamentarians" despite the new law (Buehler 2010). By tempting district heads to defraud the district budget, campaign debts thus encourage the formation of coalitions among the executive, assembly, bureaucracy, and local business contractors. Not coincidentally, in many cases a district head's creditors come from these same groups, further cementing the coalition. Officials can choose not to cooperate, but district heads who fail to fashion a manageable coalition usually get replaced by candidates who do. Although the mechanism is informal, the high cost of campaigning ensures that many district heads remain horizontally accountable to their local political allies.

The central government holds broad powers of vertical oversight. The independent central government auditing agency (Badan Pemeriksaan Keuangan, BPK) reviews district finances every year. The public prosecutor's office (Kejaksaan) and the central anticorruption agency (Komisi Pemberantasan Korupsi, KPK) have the authority to pursue criminal investigations for corruption (Davidson 2007). In early 2011, 155 corruption investigations of executives throughout Indonesia were ongoing or recently concluded (*Kompas*, January 18, 2011). Furthermore, most districts depend on block grants from the Ministry of Finance for annual revenues. Finally, the Ministry of Finance and the Ministry of Home Affairs monitor local legislation and can strike down local laws judged to contravene national ones.

> *In early 2011, 155 corruption investigations of executives throughout Indonesia were ongoing or recently concluded*

In sum, accountability mechanisms pressure district heads to conspire with other elites. The most stable district governments obtain the cooperation of business contractors, high level bureaucrats, and a majority of the district assembly. When elected officials are in debt, they must fashion a ruling coalition that includes these groups if they hope to get elected, pay off their campaign debts, and pursue reelection. It is not individual "little kings" who are corrupt, but collusion across the political class.

Three Types of Coalitions

At least three types of coalitions facilitate political collusion at the local level. This study presents political mafias, party machines, and mobilizing coalitions as Weberian ideal types, although in practice they change over time and exhibit features of multiple types. Nevertheless, conceptualizing ideal types is a useful tool for analyzing the resources and interests that animate real-world coalitions.

Local political mafias

Mafias can only exist when they control local state institutions. Coalition members—business contractors, assembly members, high-level bureaucrats, and the district head—cooperate to extract financial resources from the local bureaucracy and the annual budget. In districts where forestry and plantation agriculture is lucrative, they also manipulate land concessions. Members divide the spoils among themselves to maintain the coalition and use the remainder to contest elections. The coalition is oriented horizontally because it is limited to members of the local elite. So called "youth groups" typically participate as business contractors and assembly members (Ryter 2009).

This study uses the term mafia in a broader sense than organized racketeering, but the usage is not without precedent. First, Indonesians themselves use the term. Second, in the literature on Indonesia, McCarthy (2002, 93) and Sidel (2004, 60) have both used the term to refer to local power networks that combine politics and illegal activities. The broader literature on Southeast Asia, too, has frequently compared local politicians to mafiosi (Sidel 1999, 150–153; Ockey 2000).[5] Finally, the criminal connotation is not wholly undeserved: many local political figures do in fact combine politics with organized criminal activity, such as illegal logging, graft, and bookmaking.

Mafias extract patronage from the district budget in a variety of ways, the most important being the project tender process. In addition, district heads embezzle from the district budget directly. The budget line for social aid expenses (*belanjaan bantuan sosial*) is particularly vulnerable to embezzlement because charitable projects are not audited except to confirm disbursement. A third method of fraud involves skimming the interest from funds deposited in provincial banks.

The district head's control over bureaucratic appointments presents opportunities to extract money by selling positions. This occurs at all levels of the local bureaucracy, but the price of the bribe rises with the pay scale. Selling high-ranking positions undermines the mafia coalition, however, because agency directors who have purchased their positions will be less inclined to cooperate with the district head than those who were appointed for their loyalty.

By circulating state patronage among a narrow faction of local elites, mafias achieve a stable equilibrium between the value of available patronage and the cost of maintaining the coalition, except in election years. Popular elections strain the coalition in two ways. First, national election law requires that candidates obtain nomination from a party or coalition of parties representing 15 percent of the electorate in a given district. Although candidates may run independently, very high costs ensure that few attempt it and fewer succeed (Buehler 2010, 273–4). Second, candidates must muster a plurality of voters to win the election. Both requirements introduce huge costs. It has been widely reported that Indonesian political parties auction candidate nominations to the highest bidder (Buehler and Tan 2007, 67). Once they procure a nomination, mafia candidates resort to vote-buying as the fastest means of raising popular support.

Although corrupt campaign practices are alarming, mafias resort to vote-buying and bribing parties out of weakness. Because they are so narrow, mafias must spend more than machines to obtain a party nomination and more than mobilizing coalitions to buy votes. Mafias rely too heavily on local executive patronage. This weakness is particularly debilitating when party machines use provincial or central influence to remove district heads by denying them nomination or seeing to it that they are prosecuted for corruption.

Party machines

Party machines extract local resources as deftly as political mafias, but they draw additional strength from Indonesia's highly centralized parties, which enjoy influence over and access to provincial and central state institutions. Machines will be most influential in provinces where one party dominates the provincial government. By combining party organizational resources, the legislative functions of local and provincial assemblies, and the power

Machines will be most influential in provinces where one party dominates the provincial government

of appointment over bureaucratic institutions, machines can attack the vulnerabilities of a mafia even without significant local support. In most districts, however, machines also benefit from the support of party allies in the local bureaucracy and assembly. Machines are oriented vertically upward, because they link local officials with party power at higher levels of the Indonesian state.

Indonesian party machines fit Susan Stokes's (2005, 315) definition: "political machines (or clientelist parties) mobilize electoral support by trading particularistic benefits to voters in exchange for their votes."

Machine candidates seek electoral support through personalized offers of vote-buying and patronage. Even if they distribute these payments without the help of grassroots party organizations, party organizations help generate the resources. Furthermore, party organizations do help some candidates distribute vote payments through their affiliated youth wings. In sum, this study argues that some parties are becoming increasingly involved in efforts to mobilize voters, so much so that it is reasonable to speak of emerging party machines. Political mafias, however, do not meet the criteria of the definition because parties are less involved.

Golkar is the party with the most influence in the provincial bureaucracy of North Sumatra because of decades of nearly uninterrupted control over the governor's office.[6] In particular, the governor's prerogative to reassign civil servants enables him or her to move party loyalists to strategic positions within the provincial bureaucracy. This power is crucial in new districts and whenever district heads fail to finish a term because the governor appoints acting heads (*penjabat bupati*) endowed with full executive powers. An acting head can divert patronage away from mafias and ensure that sympathetic commissioners coordinate a new district's inaugural election.

Golkar's legislative power, though limited, reinforces the party's bureaucratic power in North Sumatra. In the fragmented provincial assembly, Golkar's faction is big enough to give it leverage over legislation, while its influence within the executive branch makes it a necessary parliamentary coalition member. When parties in the provincial assembly collude to share patronage, a phenomenon Slater (2004) has highlighted at the national level, Golkar benefits. During the legislative term 2004–2009, Golkar held 19 out of 85 seats in a provincial assembly that included 14 parties. The second-largest party, Indonesian Democratic Party of Struggle, (Partai Demokrasi Indonesia–Perjuangan, PDI-P), had 13 seats. In 2009, Golkar won only 13 seats, well behind the Democrat Party's (Partai Demokrat) 27, but still ahead of the other 13 parties represented in the expanded 100 seat legislature.

Its legislative influence also allows Golkar to manipulate the creation of new districts. Proposals to create new districts by subdividing existing districts must gain legislative approval in district, provincial, and central assemblies. This allows the major parties to draw new districts which benefit them and handicap local rivals.

Golkar's organizational power strengthens machines in the districts through candidate-nomination procedures and the disciplinary right of recall. Central party boards in Jakarta ultimately select district head candidates. While they may often sell nominations, they can also vet prospective candidates to ensure that party loyalists run in important districts. The right of recall enables parties to strip sitting assembly members of their positions by revoking their party memberships. When they are denied the support of their nominating party, assembly members lose their seats, and the party enjoys the privilege of appointing their replacements. The right of recall gives machine executives leverage over assembly members, potentially reducing the cost of obtaining legislative cooperation (Hadi Shubhan 2006).

Although Indonesian parties interpenetrate the bureaucracy and comprise the legislatures, it is important to note that parties, governors, and provincial assemblies do not possess formal authority over the Indonesian state's centralized instruments of coercion: the police and armed forces. Not even Golkar can presume the political support of men and women in uniform (Honna 2009).

Like the police and armed forces, the public prosecutor's office is a centralized bureaucracy formally insulated from partisan politics. However, parties with informal access to the provincial prosecutor (*kejati*) may exploit the institution's hierarchy to pressure district prosecutors (*kejari*) to investigate political mafias. Though mafias also seek to politicize the prosecutor's docket, they are at a disadvantage because district prosecutors answer to their provincial superiors, not the district head.

In sum, party machines have recourse to institutional resources that mafias lack. These reduce the costs of candidate nominations and cooperation between the district head and assembly. They enable machines to hinder opponents with bureaucratic reassignments, district partitioning, and, in some cases, legal action, and they provide access to a larger pool of patronage because provincial allies earmark projects for machine districts. When machines face electoral challenges, provincial patronage helps them to develop a broad coalition, further reducing costs by decreasing their dependence on vote-buying to attract electoral support.

Mobilizing coalitions

Any elite coalition can involve electoral mobilization, but playing mass politics changes the nature of a coalition. When local mafias or party machines face the prospect of losing power, they sometimes reach out to existing social organizations or mobilize new groups of voters. The strongest mobilizing coalitions emerge in districts where competing elite coalitions are evenly matched and dense social networks and well-developed organizations already exist. If mobilized social groups are routinized into durable organizations, they join the existing coalition and pressure it to respond to their needs and expectations. Mobilizing coalitions are thus oriented vertically downward because they connect political elites with larger and more diffuse social groups.

What distinguishes mobilizing coalitions, which may and often do utilize money and intimidation, from the other types is the collective nature of support for the coalition. Instead of distributing favors on a personal basis, mobilizing coalitions promise policies that more broadly benefit groups of supporters, such as ethnic or occupational groups. Consequently, they have a broader popular base than mafias or machines,

> *Instead of distributing favors on a personal basis, mobilizing coalitions promise policies that more broadly benefit groups of supporters*

but the coalition is also more expensive to maintain. Not only must elites provide benefits to whole groups instead of single individuals, but to the extent that those groups were previously excluded from receiving patronage, they place entirely new demands on the regime's resource base.

Politicians in North Sumatra offer a combination of three basic incentives to attract social groups to a mobilizing coalition. First, politicians appeal to national, ethnic, religious, or community identities to convince groups that they will advance their collectively perceived interests. Second, incumbent politicians distribute group-oriented patronage. Finally, opposition coalitions without access to state patronage may promise public goods. Mobilizing coalitions may experience intense pressure to deliver on these promises once in office.

Mobilization typically occurs via the mediation of well-developed organizations because they already command a following, understand how to organize collective action, and possess the capacity to distribute patronage. In North Sumatra, NGOs and youth groups most often play the role, but religious and cultural associations are also prominent mobilizers. Organized labor rarely, if ever, does so, although pro-labor NGOs do (Hadiz 2010, 145-60; Ford 2009).

Because expanding the coalition entails high costs, local politicians countenance it only as a last resort. Whenever possible, elites choose strategies such as vote-buying or fear mongering that mobilize voters without organizing them. The 2010 Medan mayoral election provides a striking illustration of this (Aspinall, et al. 2011). These strategies, however, are unreliable because they are based on single transactions or fleeting fears. Organizing, by contrast, institutionalizes relationships between social groups and the coalition.

Organization of the Study

In the following sections, this study highlights the contests between elite coalitions in three districts in North Sumatra, while the conclusion situates the study within the province more generally and discusses the implications for decentralization and democracy.

In 2010, political mafias fared poorly at the polls and were replaced in many places by Golkar candidates. If they did not open the coalition to new members, either popular groups or the encroaching machines, mafias could not resist challenges that deployed the combined resources of central parties, provincial bureaucracies, and legislative influence. However, the competition between mafias and machines drew previously excluded social groups into local politics. This change for more inclusive politics will endure to the extent that mobilized groups are able to continue to exert pressure on their political leaders. Whether they will depends on whether local politics remain competitive despite the decline of the mafias.

Labuhan Batu: Mafias and Mobilization

Political contention in Labuhan Batu district exemplifies the resource pressures that make local mafias unstable, even when they do not contend against party machines. Even though no Golkar machine challenged it, the district's incumbent mafia collapsed in 2008, midway through its second term in office, amid squabbles over the the spoils of office. The two resulting factions adopted starkly contrasting approaches to the 2010 district elections, but neither was able to reconstitute a durable coalition. The limited pool of state patronage and the challenges of direct elections strained each version of the mafia and made politics unpredictable as successive coalitions failed.

Although no mafia fully succeeded, the outcome of the 2010 election illustrates that a campaign strategy of mobilization can defeat the techniques referred to as "money politics." When the incumbent mafia splintered, the resulting factions neatly divided local institutions. The district head, Milwan, maintained his grip on the bureaucracy, while his opponents were a clique of businessmen and district assembly members.

> *The 2010 election illustrates that a campaign strategy of mobilization can defeat the "money politics"*

Their contrasting positions shaped their respective campaign strategies. Milwan leaned on the civil service to support his wife, Adlina, as a proxy candidate and spent an enormous amount of money to secure party nominations and buy votes. The opposition defeated Adlina decisively by mobilizing an extensive campaign network with the help of local youth groups and NGOs. The logic of money politics ultimately undid incumbent Milwan and his wife.

Located at the southern end of the plantation belt that parallels Sumatra's east coast, Labuhan Batu and its sister districts, Labuhan Batu Utara and Labuhan Batu Selatan, produce the most palm oil and rubber in North Sumatra by far (Disbun Sumut 2004a, 2004b). Steadily rising global palm oil prices have made these districts some of the province's wealthiest as measured by gross regional product and gross product per capita (BPS Sumut 2009, Table 11.3.1; Table 11.3.3). To be sure, the estates industry is dominated by large private and state-owned firms, but about one-quarter of the land devoted to palm oil and three-quarters of the land devoted to rubber are smallholdings, suggesting that small farmers also benefit from the present boom.

For a district with vast plantations, Labuhan Batu is surprisingly urban. Its overall population density ranks in the top half of the province and residents are further concentrated in the district capital Rantauprapat, where over one-third of registered voters live (BPS Sumut 2009, Table 1.1.3; KPU Labuhanbatu 2010). Several youth groups have active chapters and politically influential leaders. Ethnic associations, particularly Javanese and Chinese, command wide followings within their communities. And various NGOs serve farmers, plantation laborers, and children, among others.

Historical legacies have disarticulated labor and the traditional nobility, however. Some of North Sumatra's worst violence during the Indonesian Revolution occurred in Labuhan Batu, where five ruling houses were attacked and dozens of family members killed in March 1946 (Reid 1979). Twenty years later, organized labor was also silenced when the communist labor union, SARBUPRI (Sarekat Buruh Perkebunan Republik Indonesia [Union of Indonesian Plantation Workers]) was violently destroyed at the beginning of the New Order (Stoler 1985). Evidence once again suggests that violence was at its worst in Labuhan Batu, where killing squads in Rantauprapat filled nightly quotas (Tsai and Kammen 2012).

Milwan's Mafia

For the first ten years of the post-reform era, a former army colonel named Milwan towered over Labuhan Batu's local politics. He became district head when the assembly selected him in the 2000 indirect elections and he governed the district during two five-year terms. His distinguished military career, his success as an administrator, and Labuhan Batu's booming economy gave him sufficient stature that the local press fancied him a "national player." He was ambitious and in 2007 he made an abortive gubernatorial bid. He successfully entered provincial politics in 2010 when he was elected chair of the North Sumatra board of the Democrat Party.

The army assisted Milwan in the transition from uniformed to civilian office by posting him to Medan in 1998 (KPU Labuhanbatu 2006, 55–69). The final posting, as deputy assistant for personnel in the regional military command, carried a promotion to colonel and returned him to his home province just before the first district elections of the post-reform era. He resigned from the post in 2000 to take up the executive office in Labuhan Batu.

While in office, Milwan accumulated political power through control of the district budget, power over the local bureaucracy, and collusive relationships with business contractors and assembly members. In other words, Milwan led a local mafia that grew rich by accepting kickbacks, selling positions, and embezzling money. According to one report, project commissions during Milwan's administration exceeded 10 percent. To pay the fee, contractors inflated procurement costs by as much as 50 percent (Harahap 2008). *Bupati* Milwan preferred extravagant projects such as a sports complex in Rantauprapat that took 13 years to build and cost nearly Rp 15 billion (US$1.6 million)

> *Milwan led a local mafia that grew rich by accepting kickbacks, selling positions, and embezzling money*

(Harahap 2009). A recent investigation implicated Adlina, Milwan's wife, in an organized syndicate that was accepting payments for bureaucratic appointments (*Metro Rantau*, October 14, 2010). Finally, the administration embezzled money directly from the district budget. The central audit board noted irregularities in district financial reporting during fiscal years 2004, 2005, and 2006, prompting one local newspaper to proclaim, "Audit findings: Millions of rupiah of Labuhan Batu district funds evaporate" (*Waspada Online*, May 28, 2008).

The mafia included associates in many local institutions, particularly construction contractors, youth group leaders, assembly members, bureaucrats, and Golkar. Fredy Simangunsong, a business contractor and leader of the local chapter of the youth group named Functional Youth League (Ikatan Pemuda Karya, IPK), was Milwan's most prominent ally. Fredy claims to have received contracts worth Rp 11 billion (US$1.2 million) in 2006 and Rp 24 billion (US$2.6 million) in 2007, while paying kickbacks totaling Rp 1.6 billion (US$175,000) (*Sinar Indonesia Baru*, November 4, 2008). Fredy's wife, Elya Rosa Siregar, sat in the district assembly as a member of the Golkar delegation. She and her assembly colleagues cooperated with Milwan to the extent that they approved each budget and financial report. A member of the 1999–2004 assembly from PDI-P, Daslan Simandjuntak, recently testified before the central anticorruption agency that he accepted bribes of Rp 30 million (US$3,000) to pass those bills (*Ini Medan Bung*, February 10, 2011). Three bureaucratic agencies were singled out in the central audit board's reports of financial irregularities: health (Dinas

Kesehatan), education (Dinas Pendidikan), and settlement and infrastructure (Dinas Permukiman dan Prasarana Daerah). It is likely that the directors of these agencies were close allies of the mafia.

Golkar's role in the mafia deserves special mention to demonstrate that Milwan's coalition was not a party machine. Since retiring from his military career in 2000, Milwan has been opportunistic in his dealings with parties. In 2005, he was elected to lead the local chapter of Golkar. During the peak of the mafia's power, the chairmanship helped Milwan negotiate with the district assembly and offered a tantalizing chance at the gubernatorial nomination. Milwan did not, however, win Golkar's endorsement for governor for the 2008 election, and he subsequently looked elsewhere for a nomination. He was linked to both Democrat Party and United Development Party (Partai Persatuan Pembangunan, PPP), much to the annoyance of Golkar's provincial leaders, who sacked him in November 2007 (*Waspada Online*, November 22, 2007). Though Golkar still nominated Adlina during the 2010 district election, it was but 1 of 28 parties to do so and many local members resented the decision. Only five months after Adlina lost, Milwan became the chair of Democrat's provincial board. He exemplifies the independent politician who purchases nominations and opportunistically switches parties, as described by Mietzner (2009b).

> *[Milwan] exemplifies the independent politician who purchases nominations and opportunistically switches parties*

The Mafia Collapses

In 2008, Milwan lost control of the mafia and it collapsed into two competing factions. Milwan's faction retained control over the local bureaucracy by virtue of his continuing term in executive office. This faction also maintained relationships with various ethnic associations, particularly the Javanese migrant organization Pujakesuma (Putra Jawa Kelahiran Sumatera, [Sons of Java Born in Sumatra]). Pujakesuma's local chairperson, Sudarwanto, served as deputy head in Milwan's administration.

The opposing faction was directed by a clique of powerful business contractors known locally as "the mafia." Fredy Simangunsong was the most outspoken of the clique, but Ramli Siahaan, Tutur Parapat, and Sujian (perhaps better known as Acan) were equal partners in the opposition. Each of these men, except Acan, combined business contracting and plantation ownership with youth group leadership. Acan possessed similar business interests but was not affiliated with a youth group. Instead, he was a prominent leader in Rantauprapat's Chinese community.[7] Although the plantation tycoon D.L. Sitorus was not as personally involved in local politics, he supported this group as well. His party, the National People's Concern Party (Partai Peduli Rakyat Nasional) endorsed the opposition candidate, Tigor Siregar, during the 2010 election, contributing two vital seats toward the 15 percent nomination threshold.

To the alliance of business contractors and youth groups, the opposition faction added an assertive presence in the district assembly and support from some NGOs. Fredy's wife, Elya Rosa Siregar, led a legislative contingent that claimed the sympathies of members from both of the two largest factions, Golkar and PDI-P, as well as from a number of smaller parties. Their influence turned the assembly against Milwan. After the 2009 general elections Elya Rosa became chair (Ketua DPRD), and its hostility toward the district head intensified further. Finally, the opposition selected Suhari Pane, former chair of the election commission and longtime NGO activist, as its candidate for deputy head in 2010. Suhari's network among activists extended from farmers' to women's organizations and lent credibility to the ticket's promises of better government.

While the immediate reasons for the mafia's collapse are vague, the underlying pressures that weakened it are clear enough. Milwan and Fredy were bickering about money. Milwan needed money if he was to realize his dream of becoming governor. Fredy owed Milwan approximately Rp 1 billion in kickbacks (US $105,000) and complained that the graft was becoming exorbitant (*Labuhanbatu News*, October 27, 2008). Meanwhile, it was rumored that Elya Rosa was at the time considering a bid for district head, and Milwan likely felt Fredy was becoming too powerful a rival.[8] Regardless of the particulars of the disagreement, Milwan's mafia succumbed to a political dilemma. Two of its most important fundraising techniques, collecting project kickbacks and selling bureaucratic positions, alienated the contractors and bureaucrats upon whose cooperation the coalition depended.

In October 2008, the rift became public when the animosity between Milwan and Fredy boiled over. On October 16, Fredy aired the details of his business dealings with Milwan in a press conference. He announced that he intended to press charges and promised that he and his associates would join the opposition. The press conference touched off a series of public battles that culminated in Adlina's defeat in the 2010 district election (*Sinar Indonesia Baru*, November 4, 2008).

The press conference was Fredy's retaliation after he had been dismissed from the district chairmanship of the youth organization IPK. He accused Milwan of interfering with the provincial leadership to have him sacked. Milwan was right to fear the position because IPK's young, underemployed membership represented a pool of cheap labor, a muscular force for street politics, and a vehicle for political organizing. Although Fredy never recovered the chairmanship, his friend Ramli incorporated a local chapter of a new youth group, MPI (Masyarakat Pancasila Indonesia), on April 4, 2009. Fredy and Tutur Parapat attended the opening ceremony, and the new organization would become a key part of the opposition faction's electoral campaign against Adlina (*Sinar Indonesia Baru*, April 11, 2009).

A controversy protesting the reassignment of over one hundred school headmasters provided the opposition faction its best opportunity to attack Milwan. In 2008, shortly after a routine bureaucratic rotation, hundreds of headmasters filed a police report alleging that an unnamed official was soliciting bribes in exchange for a promise of exemption from reassignment. The headmasters then formally complained to the district assembly, where Milwan's foes enthusiastically took up the complaint (*Labuhanbatu News*, August 7, 2008). Not only did the controversy force Milwan to pay out bribes to quiet his critics in the assembly, but it also damaged Adlina's reputation because of her alleged involvement.[9]

In August, the assembly deliberated to pass approval of 2008 budget spending. Elya Rosa was particularly outspoken on this occasion. She called attention to budget items with large amounts of unspent funds, and she complained that social programs were administered by the district women's organization (Pemberdayaan Kesejahteraan Keluarga, PKK), which was chaired by Adlina (*Sinar Indonesia Baru*, August 30, 2009).

Even the completion of one of Milwan's signature construction projects in November 2009 prompted criticism. After 13 years of delays and accidents, the district finally completed what was billed as North Sumatra's biggest and best sports complex. The opening was jeered, however, because of the project's enormous cost of Rp 14.9 billion (US$1.6 million). The week it opened, cracks appeared in the back wall of the building (*Sinar Indonesia Baru*, November 20, 2009).

> *Milwan's mega-projects, very profitable in terms of graft, became major sources of embarrassment that voters remembered on polling day*

Even with the sports complex complete, two other mega-projects were still behind schedule. A market complex and a bus terminal would not be finished before the 2010 election. Milwan's mega-projects, very profitable in terms of graft, became major sources of embarrassment that voters remembered on polling day.

Money Politics and Mobilization in the 2010 District Election

The contest between the competing factions of the mafia was ultimately resolved by the 2010 district election. Milwan, having already served the limit of two terms, advanced Adlina as a candidate together with a Pujakesuma functionary named Trisno. Fredy's faction chose to support a respected medical doctor named Tigor Siregar and the aforementioned Suhari Pane. Each side conducted campaign strategy to take greatest advantage of its organizational sources of power. Milwan's approach exemplified "money politics." He expended billions of rupiah on party nominations, voter handouts, and favorable press coverage. He expected his organizational allies—Pujakesuma and the bureaucracy—to deliver their constituencies on election day. By contrast, the opposition mobilized a network of campaign volunteers that brought thousands of new voters to the polls. The strategy built on existing youth group and NGO networks and employed those activists in the organizational effort. Fredy and his youth group allies capably deployed negative campaign tactics, as well. The mobilization effort paid off for the opposition, as Tigor-Suhari won the election with 53 percent of the vote compared to 38 percent for Adlina (KPU Sumut 2010b).

Adlina's campaign

At the outset, Milwan and Adlina were strong favorites. Adlina's position as the chair of the women's organization allowed her to begin her campaign a year early. Since the organization administered social projects, Adlina toured villages distributing oil palm and corn seedlings, fertilizer, and mosquito nets. She passed out headscarves and sacks of rice marked with a heart, her campaign symbol, and accompanied by a message from Ibu PKK (Madame PKK) (*Sinar Indonesia Baru*, August 30, 2009).

While Adlina campaigned, Milwan moved to sideline Tigor. In March 2009, Milwan removed Tigor from his position as director of Rantauprapat Public Hospital (*Metro Rantau*, November 12, 2009). Tigor made the most of the unwanted dismissal by spending the rest of the year traveling around the district performing free circumcisions. He believes the volunteer work increased his popularity and earned him votes in 2010.[10]

> **While Adlina campaigned, Milwan moved to sideline Tigor**

Milwan expected much from the bureaucracy. Civil servants in the lower levels of the bureaucracy, such as ward (*lurah*), subdistrict (*camat*) and popularly elected village heads (*kepala desa*), were of particular importance. They exercised de facto discretion over the distribution of government development programs within their jurisdictions, and thus had the capacity to politicize state patronage. Government programs, for example a free identity-card-processing scheme, became campaign events (*Ini Medan Bung*, January 31, 2010). In addition, subdistrict offices composed a short-list of candidates for election logistics committees (*panitia pemilihan kecamatan*, PPK), allowing them to ensure that Milwan's partisans oversaw election preparations, logistics, and vote-counting. However, there is little evidence that the logistics committees made a concerted effort to manipulate the election results, despite some reports of problems at the polls.

The primary tool for manipulating the bureaucracy was the executive's right to reassign civil servants. Between March and May 2009, Milwan reassigned or confirmed nearly 300 civil servants at all levels of the bureaucracy, from the district secretary (*sekretaris daerah*, or *sekda*) to village heads. By doing so, he filled the bureaucracy's strategic positions with his supporters before the election and served notice that he would not hesitate to reassign disloyal civil servants.

By her own count, 28 political parties backed Adlina's campaign. Some of the parties, however, made no effort to deliver their constituencies after conferring their nomination. Milwan may have anticipated the problem early in the campaign when he challenged them, saying "the success of this campaign will reflect the self-respect [*harga diri*] of the parties, because the coalition supporting Adlina-Trisno is very large" (*Waspada*, March 23, 2010). Party loyalties were divided, with Golkar as a case in point. Fredy and Elya Rosa both held local party office and criticized Adlina and Milwan in Golkar's name, while Governor Syamsul Arifin campaigned on their behalf (*Metro Rantau*, June 14, 2010). In all likelihood, local activists from Golkar as well as other parties felt little loyalty to Adlina because Milwan purchased the nominations by making financial donations to central and provincial party boards.

Adlina's party strategy made it difficult for Tigor to fashion a coalition of parties representing the requisite 15 percent of the electorate. Adlina's coalition included the major parties—Democrat, Golkar, PDI-P, Welfare and Justice Party (Partai Keadilan Sejahtera, PKS), and National Mandate Party (Partai Amanat Nasional)—and accounted for 35 out of 50 seats in the assembly. Tigor was left to fashion a coalition with the minimum of 8 assembly seats around PPP. It was rumored that Adlina's team tried and failed to lure away one of Tigor's supporting parties at the eleventh hour.[11] If the gambit had succeeded Tigor might have been disqualified for failing to meet the nomination threshold. Adlina's strategy also included a third candidate. Irfan, a retired civil servant, ran as an independent. He campaigned little and performed poorly at the polls. Nevertheless, had Milwan prevented Tigor from registering as a candidate, Irfan would have provided legitimacy to an uncontested election, much as "escorting candidates" (*calon pendamping*) did during the New Order (Malley 1999, 86). Even after Tigor was nominated, Milwan contributed financially to Irfan's campaign in an effort to split the opposition vote.[12]

In addition to leaning on the bureaucracy and political parties, the campaign reached out to civil society via ethnic associations and the press. Of the ethnic associations, Pujakesuma was most important because Javanese comprise 44.8 percent of the combined population in

Labuhan Batu, Labuhan Batu Utara, and Labuhan Batu Selatan (Batubara 2009). However, just as Aspinall et al. (2011) demonstrated with respect to Medan's 2010 election, Javanese did not vote as a single bloc. Milwan paid the local newspapers to shower favorable coverage on Adlina's campaign. The partisanship of the local *Metro Rantau* was particularly bald, but it was not alone.

The linchpin of Milwan and Adlina's campaign was the attempt to buy votes directly. As early as 2009, Adlina handed out money for transport to health workers, as gifts for teachers, and as honorariums for campaign workers. During the campaign proper, she paid motorcycle taxi drivers to escort campaign processions. And like campaign teams throughout North Sumatra, her team passed out Rp 50,000 notes (about US$6) on the eve of the election in what is commonly called "the attack at dawn" (*serangan fajar*) (*Ini Medan Bung*, December 7, 2009; *Sinar Indonesia Baru*, June 14, 2010a).

> *The linchpin of Milwan and Adlina's campaign was the attempt to buy votes directly*

Add all of the campaign expenditures up, and Milwan and Adlina's campaign cost an extraordinary amount of money. Local observers enjoy speculating as to the amount, with guesses ranging wildly from Rp 10 billion to 100 billion (US$1.1 million–11 million). Regardless of the actual amount, it seems clear that Milwan and Adlina outspent Tigor in a classic campaign of money politics. From party nominations to vote-buying, they believed their money would purchase support. The case would support Hadiz's (2003) criticism that Indonesian democracy is vulnerable to elite capture through money politics—except that in this case, Adlina lost.

Tigor's campaign

Tigor's campaign strategy focused on face-to-face contact between the candidates, campaign volunteers, and voters. Though this campaign, like Adlina's, likely involved gift giving, payments occurred within the context of a concerted attempt to organize supporters. Tigor and his running mate Suhari stumped, but the number of people they encountered touring was naturally limited. To extend the message, the campaign team developed a large network of volunteers. The goal was to recruit 20 volunteers in every village and ward in the entire district. The campaign team placed five operatives in every subdistrict for the purpose of recruiting volunteers. At the end of the campaign, Tigor boasted that 12,000 volunteers had registered with his team and worked on the campaign. These volunteers became responsible for the campaign in their respective villages. They arranged logistics and extended invitations to the candidates to make campaign stops in their villages.[13]

Tigor's plan to establish chapters of campaign volunteers in every town and village followed the model of North Sumatra's youth organizations, and Tigor's campaign team interpenetrated those organizations. The most important of them was Ramli's MPI, but members of other organizations also cooperated with Ramli and Fredy to support Tigor's campaign. It is likely that these groups provided the operatives to recruit village volunteers. However, their work was easier because Tigor and Suhari were well known in Labuhan Batu's villages because of their charitable work there, Tigor as a doctor and Suhari as a farmers' advocate.

In the villages, Tigor presented an agenda of public goods (*Metro Rantau*, September 2, 2010). He talked about improving health services and education, and his bread-and-butter issue was identity cards. He insisted that the bureaucracy should process these free of charge and promised that if elected he would see to it that they were. The promise appealed to all classes of voters and indirectly criticized the lower level bureaucrats upon whom Adlina's campaign depended, since village and ward leaders were the ones who processed identity cards and collected processing fees.

Tigor's backers—Fredy, Ramli, and their associates—also waged an aggressively negative campaign. One early attack against Adlina accused her of submitting a false high school diploma to the district election commission (*Sinar Indonesia Baru*, April 13, 2010). All executive candidates must hold a high school diploma, so the allegation simultaneously challenged her right to run for office and defamed her character. In addition, the opposition taunted Adlina by hanging insulting banners around the district, some of which were "signed" with Fredy's name. One read, "Thank you Mrs. Adlina for the rice and money, but we still prefer Tigor" (*Metro Rantau*, May 31, 2010).

The election results indicated that Tigor, Suhari, Fredy, Elya Rosa, Ramli, and the others successfully mobilized voters to oppose Adlina and Milwan. Adlina received only 72,000 votes, nearly 14,000 fewer votes than her husband had achieved in 2005 in the part of Labuhan Batu that was not later partitioned. In contrast, Tigor's ticket received over 100,000 votes, an increase of 28,000 voters over the combined opposition total in the previous election. The figures suggest that not only did Tigor's campaign attract voters who had previously supported Milwan, but it also persuaded thousands of new voters to choose Tigor. In all, turnout in 2010 increased by 21,000 votes and voter registration by nearly 40,000 people. The election data are highly consistent with the contention that Tigor's team carried out an effective get-out-the-vote campaign (KPU Labuhanbatu 2006, Appendix 1; 2010).

> **Turnout in 2010 increased by 21,000 votes and voter registration by nearly 40,000 people**

As successful as the mobilization effort was on election day, it placed great strain on the opposition coalition afterwards. Campaign promises had raised hopes so high, and the opposition encompassed so many diverse groups, that when Tigor and Suhari were inaugurated disillusionment set in almost immediately. The criticism focused on the incompatible interests of Fredy and the business contractors—who intended to reconstitute the mafia—and of the villagers, volunteers, and voters—who hoped for efficient implementation of Tigor's programs.

Tigor's fate was tied to Fredy and the mafia because he owed his position to them. The opening ceremony for Milwan's mega-project, Padang Bulan Bus Terminal, illustrated the power of the "new" mafia. After 12 years of construction, the new facility would increase district revenues, improve traffic flow, and beautify Rantauprapat. The opening was the most important event of Tigor's young administration. Having been humiliated by the campaign against his wife, Milwan did not attend though he had managed the project for years. Instead, Tigor and deputy Suhari proudly presided. Standing beside them were Fredy, Elya Rosa, and Ramli (*Metro Rantau*, September 3, 2010).

However, it is unlikely that the mafia will maintain such a united image for long. Having mobilized so many volunteers, it will be very difficult for Tigor to satisfy all of his constituents. The first cracks appeared on October 1, 2010, when a scandal erupted because Tigor was accused of pressuring the oceans and fisheries agency (Dinas Perikanan dan Kelautan) to award a project tender to one of his campaign supporters (*Metro Rantau*, October 1, 2010).

Milwan's mafia collapsed when the patronage resources available at the district level proved insufficient to satisfy both him and Fredy. While the spoils of office have remained constant, the pressure on the political mafia is greater than ever because the new administration must answer to 10,000 campaign volunteers who mobilized to defeat Milwan. It will be extremely difficult to maintain such a large coalition.

Tapanuli Selatan: A Mafia against a Machine

Tapanuli Selatan's politics during the post-reform era illustrate the full life cycle, so to speak, of a political mafia. The case shows how decentralization reform allowed mafias to emerge, and how counterreform contributed to their decline and eventual eclipse by a party machine. Shortly after the collapse of the New Order, a "timber mafia" coalesced in Tapanuli Selatan by monopolizing the lucrative logging and plantation concessions that Law No. 22/1999 appeared to place under the authority of local governments. The mafia came to exercise a great deal of influence over many local institutions, particularly the executive and legislative branches of government, the judiciary, the election commission, and Golkar's district chapter. Even after national legislation revoked local authority to manage forests, the mafia remained powerful without its raison d'être because it retained its institutional allies. In this way, it resisted the encroachment of the Golkar machine for several years before finally succumbing. In order to prevail, the machine used its provincial and central influence to ensure that the subdivision of the district would marginalize the mafia's electoral base.

The district is among North Sumatra's most remote, rural, and poorest. Despite rich forests, mineral deposits, and plantations, Tapanuli Selatan's per capita income remains low, at Rp 7.2 million (US$790) in 2007 (BPS Sumut 2009, Table 11.3.3). Foreign and national firms dominate these main industries, leaving little opportunity for local business to develop. Consequently, social organizations are not as well established as elsewhere in the province. Labor organizations are weak, and the youth groups have few outposts in rural areas. Customary associations and clan affiliations are the most influential social networks.

District geography extends from the summits of the Bukit Barisan mountains to the coastal lowlands on the shores of the Indian Ocean, and agricultural products match the topography in variety. The highlands are cultivated in wet rice, the intermediate zones in rubber, and the lowlands in palm oil. Before it was divided into three districts in 2007, Tapanuli Selatan ranked among the top producers in the province of each of these commodities due to its enormous size (BPS Sumut 2009, Table 5.1.3; Disbun Sumut 2004a, 2004b). But natural resources are the prize of the economy. Before 2007, the district had the most forestland in North Sumatra by far. Besides timber, forested areas also contain gold deposits as well as endangered orangutans, but both the forests and fauna are disappearing fast.

The history of plantation labor in Tapanuli Selatan is quite different from Labuhan Batu or Serdang Bedagai because large-scale estates production started much later. The laboring population is composed of recent migrants from Java, Nias Island, and Tapanuli Utara and it is organized differently than in the traditional plantation belt. On many estates, workers participate in a cooperative whereby each family receives two hectares of land on the condition that it sells its produce to the concession holder. Because the estates industry was not yet established at the time, it is likely that anticommunist violence during 1965–66 was less bloody in Tapanuli Selatan than along the east coast.

Decentralization and the Rise of the Timber Mafia

In several publications, John McCarthy has described the operations of "timber mafias" composed of "clientelist coalitions" that manage lucrative logging activities in forested districts of Indonesia. During the dying days of the New Order, a mafia in Aceh Tenggara district linked the district head with "forestry staff working for the National Park, police (*Polres*) and army personnel (*Kodim*), local government officials, the judiciary and local religious leaders (*imam*)" (McCarthy 2002, 93–4). In the years immediately following decentralization reform, "district actors and administrators had exceptional opportunities to gain benefits" from timber resources because they gained authority to grant logging permits and land concessions (McCarthy 2007, 153). In Central Kalimantan's Barito Selatan district, the district head issued logging and transit permits to political allies and wealthy logging conglomerates. Members of the district assembly, journalists, and NGOs accepted pay-offs from loggers, as did a host of law enforcement agencies, including the police, the military, and forestry officials. In addition, an estimated 60 assembly members were "directly involved in timber enterprises" (Ibid., 168–9).

Evidence suggests that a similar mafia was active in Tapanuli Selatan at the same time. Certainly timber represented a very valuable resource present in the district. Shane Barter (2008, 10–11) reported that in North Sumatra, logging concessions granted by district governments increased "a thousand fold" after 1998 and he identified Saleh Harahap, district head of Tapanuli Selatan, as a primary culprit. North Sumatra's most sensational illegal logging case commenced during this period in Tapanuli Selatan when D.L. Sitorus opportunistically took possession of tens of thousands of hectares of

> *In North Sumatra, logging concessions granted by district governments increased "a thousand fold" after 1998*

forest reserve in 1998. Taking advantage of the breakdown in central authority, he bypassed the Ministry of Forestry and negotiated directly with traditional leaders who claimed to exercise customary rights (*hak ulayat*) over the land. He converted the forest to palm oil, attracting a workforce to clear and plant by giving two hectares of land to members of a cooperative (Koperasi Bukit Harapan [Mount Hope Cooperative]) which sold exclusively to him. The cooperative cultivated; Sitorus obtained documentation of land tenure. This he procured locally, in all likelihood dealing directly with district level officials at the local forestry agency (Dinas Kehutanan) and the national land tenure board (Badan Pertanahan Nasional, BPN), and, of course, with the district head (Johan, et al. 2000; Hasugian and Batubara 2005).

According to McCarthy (2007), district officials abruptly lost the power to regulate logging in 2002. He cites the newly autonomous police force and a government regulation (*Peraturan Pemerintah* No. 34/2002) that restored authority over timber permits and concessions to the Ministry of Forestry as the two main causes. As a result of these developments, district governments in Central Kalimantan relinquished control of timber rents to the provincial police and numerous district officials faced prosecution in the provincial courts. In North Sumatra, the provincial police, the public prosecutor's office, and the Ministry of Forestry similarly initiated a series of high profile illegal logging cases. In 2005, the attorney general's office charged D.L. Sitorus with corruption and illegally converting forestland. The same year, the Ministry of Forestry named Saleh Harahap an illegal logging suspect shortly before the latter's death (Baskoro, et al. 2006; Ramidi, et al. 2006).

Stalemate: The 2005 District Elections

Already strained because of the pressure from the Ministry of Forestry and provincial law enforcement officials, the mafia collapsed completely during the 2005 direct district elections. The incumbent district head, the chair of the assembly, and the district secretary—all erstwhile allies—declared candidacies during an extremely contentious campaign. D.L. Sitorus, arguably the most important businessman in the district, supported a crony in the district office of the national land tenure board (BPN) as yet another candidate. Thus four out of ten candidates who registered with the local election commission originated from the timber mafia.

> *The [timber] mafia collapsed completely during the 2005 direct district elections*

The chair of the assembly, Bachrum Harahap, was the favorite to win the election and rebuild the coalition. A real estate broker among other things, Bachrum grew rich during his time in the assembly and developed a loyal network of followers by directing projects to his friends. He also chaired the local chapter of Golkar, an important position because the party dominated both branches of local government. The district head, Saleh Harahap, was a longtime party member. In the assembly, Golkar held 14 out of 45 seats after winning nearly 30 percent of the vote in the 2004 legislative elections. By comparison, the second leading party, PPP, controlled only six seats (KPU Tapsel 2005a).

Bachrum's leadership of Golkar seemed to assure him of the party's nomination, so Saleh Harahap sought out other parties to endorse his candidacy. He asked his district secretary, Rahudman Harahap, to approach PDI-P to secure its nomination. The secretary deceived Saleh and persuaded PDI-P to support himself instead. As a result, when Saleh registered with the election committee, it disqualified him and announced Rahudman as the rightful PDI-P candidate. Saleh died a few months later, but not before exacting revenge. He reported Rahud-man to the provincial police for embezzling civil servant bonuses. Because it took so long to investigate, the case did not prevent Rahudman from running for district head (or for mayor of Medan five years later), but it did illustrate how acrimoniously the mafia collapsed (*Waspada Online*, June 29, 2009).

Even though Saleh conceded Golkar's support, Bachrum still almost lost the nomination. The threat came from Golkar's central and provincial leadership, which preferred a pairing of Herry Siregar and Chaidir Ritonga, the incumbent deputy head and Golkar's deputy treasurer for the province. The leadership knew that Bachrum would never sign a nomination letter for a rival, so it also moved to sack Bachrum from his position as district party chair.

When Bachrum realized that the party convention would not give him the nomination, he acted quickly. At 8 p.m. on April 6, 2005, two days before the registration deadline, he appeared at the election commission's office in the town of Padang Sidempuan and registered as the candidate for Golkar. His paperwork was in order and he presented all the required signatures: from himself as party chair, from the party secretary, and from both candidates on the ticket, himself and Tongku Palit Hasibuan.

Two days later, a delegation from Medan came to register the convention's choice for the Golkar nomination. They presented a letter recalling Bachrum from his position as district party chair as well as all the required signatures based on the new party hierarchy. At first, the election commission was reluctant to accept the nomination because Golkar had already submitted one nomination, but the delegation persuaded it to process both nominations and promised to await the outcome of the candidate-verification process.

Election regulations stipulated that in the event that one party nominated more than one candidate, the party's central board had the final authority to designate the candidate. At the advice of the provincial election commission, the election commission sent a letter to Golkar on May 2, 2005, requesting clarification, and a few days later the commission sent a delegation of three to Jakarta to meet with the central board face to face. The board declared that it supported Herry Siregar and Chaidir Ritonga as Golkar's candidates. Upon returning to Padang Sidempuan, the chair of the election commission,

Erwin Syarifuddin Harahap, and one member, Fitri Leniwati Harahap, signed a letter declaring Herry and Chaidir as Golkar's rightful nominee (*Sumut Pos*, May 18, 2005).

At this point, the election commission split. The three commissioners who had not signed the letter called a plenary meeting at which they used their majority to reach a number of decisions. First, they declared the letter invalid because it had not been previously agreed upon in a plenary session. Second, they repudiated the letter they had sent requesting clarification from Golkar's central board. Third, they voted to endorse Bachrum as the Golkar candidate. Fourth, they replaced the chair with one of their own, Mustar Edi Hutasuhut. Finally, they resolved to press charges of forgery and misconduct against Erwin and Fitri for their actions in support of Herry and Chaidir's candidacy (KPU Tapsel 2005b; 2005c).

News reports, local gossip, and the absurdity of some of the decisions taken by the group of three election commissioners all suggested that they were in Bachrum's pocket. Whether or not they were bribed, their loyalty to Bachrum paid off as a wise career choice. Two of them accompanied him to the new district Padang Lawas Utara, where in 2008 Bachrum became the first elected district head. M. Aman Siregar joined the election commission there while Amril Hakim Harahap received a civil service appointment in the education agency (Dinas Pendidikan). Mustar Edi, meanwhile, retained his newly acquired position as chair of Tapanuli Selatan's election commission for a second term that commenced in December 2008. By contrast, Bachrum's opponents Erwin and Fitri retired from public life at the conclusion of their terms. Fitri started an NGO that assists battered women and Erwin opened a restaurant.

> *News reports, local gossip, and the absurdity of some of the decisions taken by the group of three election commissioners all suggested that they were in Bachrum's pocket*

Mustar Edi, M. Aman, and Amril Hakim may also have feared Bachrum's reputation for vindictiveness. Despite pressure from the provincial election commission, they refused to drop the charges against Erwin and Fitri. The trial began after the election and after one hearing

Erwin and Fitri were held in contempt of court for failing to appear. They had stayed home on the advice of their lawyer. They spent the duration of the trial, nine weeks, in jail. They were eventually found guilty of forgery, the lesser charge, and sentenced to time served. The spiteful nature of the charges and the harshness of the contempt finding again suggest that the court was biased in favor of Bachrum.

Throughout the nomination process, Bachrum demonstrated his influence over local institutions. Within the district branch of Golkar, he sidelined the incumbent district head and persuaded the party secretary to cooperate with him to seize the nomination. The district election commission took his side against the recommendations of the provincial commission. It is likely that he influenced the decisions taken by the local court. Using his local connections, he outsmarted and outmuscled the provincial and central Golkar leadership and seized the nomination.

Despite his influence, Bachrum lost the election. On election day, June 27, 2005, he finished second with 22 percent of the vote. Ongku Hasibuan, a little-known mining engineer nominated by PKS and Partai Kebangkitan Bangsa (National Awakening Party), won the election with 33 percent (KPU Sumut 2005). Local observers have little doubt that the nomination fight cost Bachrum the election. During the controversy, Golkar activists drifted away to other candidates (*Media Indonesia*, May 6, 2005). Bachrum lost time on the campaign trail. The dispute cast doubt on the legitimacy of his candidacy as well as the election itself. The week before the election, no less a person than Agung Laksono, Golkar national deputy chair and chair of the national assembly (Dewan Perwakilan Rakyat, DPR), publicly declared the Tapanuli Selatan election "legally flawed" (*Waspada*, June 29, 2005a). Golkar's internal struggle over the 2005 nomination culminated in a draw, with both sides losing. Bachrum prevented the central leadership from nominating its preferred candidate, while the central leadership prevented Bachrum from winning the election.

The Mafia Counterattacks: Subdividing the District

Following his election loss, Bachrum immediately set to work drawing the lines for Tapanuli Selatan's next political battle. During the lame duck period before Ongku's inauguration, Bachrum used his influence as chair of the district assembly to pass a proposal to subdivide

Tapanuli Selatan. Bachrum's plan called for the creation of three new districts, called Angkola Sipirok, Padang Lawas, and Tapanuli Selatan (Ritonga 2008a).

Bachrum's bill proposed to make Tapanuli Selatan, where Ongku would administer, smaller and poorer than the other two districts. Of Tapanuli Selatan's 28 subdistricts, Angkola Sipirok would encompass 11, Padang Lawas 10, and Tapanuli Selatan 7. Tapanuli Selatan's proposed population was much less than that of the other districts, and the subdistricts allocated to it were more remote and less developed. Most importantly, the proposal reserved much of Tapanuli Selatan's most productive plantation land to the proposed Padang Lawas district, where Bachrum's electoral base of support resided (Hidayat 2007).

After Bachrum's proposal passed in Tapanuli Selatan's assembly on July 28, 2005, it quickly worked its way through the North Sumatra provincial government. Once the provincial assembly approved it, Governor Rudolf Pardede endorsed it on November 29, 2005, and sent it to Jakarta, where Agung Laksono and the rest of the national assembly took a full year to write it into a bill. The respite gave Bachrum's opponents an opportunity to prepare a response.

On February 1, 2007, Ongku wrote the president to explain that if Bachrum's plan passed, it would at once impoverish the district named Tapanuli Selatan and burden it with the added responsibility of financially and administratively supporting the new districts until they became fully autonomous. As a solution he proposed that Tapanuli Selatan administer the eleven subdistricts that corresponded to Bachrum's Angkola Sipirok. Padang Lawas would administer not ten subdistricts but seven, and the remaining three would shift to the third district, called Barumun Raya under Ongku's plan. These three subdistricts were chosen carefully. Two of them, Simangambat and Barumum Tengah, held vast tracts of D.L. Sitorus's palm oil plantations. The third was the location of Ongku's hometown.

The final step in Ongku's campaign was to push the revision through Bachrum's district assembly. The difficult task required shrewd maneuvering (Ritonga 2008b). Ongku's supporters in PKS announced in the local press that because of the subdivision debate, the assembly was hopelessly behind on its routine tasks. In this way, they justified calling a special meeting to create a new assembly agenda. Sometime in early April 2007 when Bachrum was away in Jakarta, Khoiruddin Siregar, one of the deputy chairs of the assembly, called a consulting commit-tee meeting (*panitia musyawarah*) that had the authority to set a new agenda. At the meeting, Khoiruddin and the PKS assembly members inserted Ongku's revised proposal into the agenda by a vote of 12 to 9 (*Waspada*, April 24, 2007).

On Friday, April 20, 2007, the assembly met to discuss the pro-posed revision. Bachrum and the other Golkar assembly members were furious. Hundreds of protesters assembled outside, but it was inside the assembly chambers where violence broke out. Before the meeting was called to or-der, Syarifuddin Hasibuan of Golkar punched Edi Hasan Nasution of PKS in the face. Syarifuddin overturned tables, shattered glass, and broke ash-trays. His actions made the

> *Inside the assembly chambers, violence broke out—Syarifuddin Hasibuan of Golkar punched Edi Hasan Nasution of PKS in the face*

chambers unusable, and the session transferred to the conference room at the district head's office. Under tight security, 26 out of 45 assembly members attended. Khoiruddin presided; Bachrum and many of his supporters were absent (*Waspada*, April 21, 2007).

The attending assembly members settled the matter the same day in a marathon session. They established a special committee to discuss the revision, which recommended approval by thirteen votes against six abstentions. The six abstaining voters were all from Golkar and had walked out of the session earlier that morning. The assembly im-mediately put the committee's recommendation to a vote. It passed Ongku's revision and declared all previous subdivision plans null and void. By the end of the day, the revised bill was on its way to the gov-ernor's office in Medan. Governor Pardede promptly approved it and by Tuesday, April 24, 2007, it had been forwarded to the Ministry of Home Affairs which prepared it for discussion in the national assembly in early May (*Waspada*, April 24, 2007).

The draft that finally reached the floor of the national assembly fol-lowed Ongku's plan but for one concession: Bachrum was able to add Simangambat subdistrict, which was the center of D.L. Sitorus's palm oil operations, to Padang Lawas Utara, the district he would eventually administer (Ritonga 2008b).

Ongku's campaign to revise the subdivision bill required a high degree of cooperation from all levels of Indonesia's government. After it passed the district assembly, the bill still needed prompt cooperation from the governor and Ministry of Home Affairs to reach the DPR in time for the session scheduled to discuss partition bills. The speed at which the bill passed through the bureaucracy is all the more remarkable when compared to the much longer amount of time it took Bachrum's bill to make the same journey. The revision effort was carefully premeditated and widely supported by district, provincial, and central officials.

The defeat of his district subdivision proposal further diminished Bachrum's influence in Tapanuli Selatan. His ally in the assembly, Syarifuddin, was sentenced to six months in prison for his violent actions in the assembly chambers (*Waspada Online*, September 29, 2007). Padang Lawas Utara was the smallest of the three new districts. When Bachrum became district head there the following year, he resigned his position as chair of Tapanuli Selatan's assembly and removed himself from a formal role in district politics. After 2005, he never recovered his position as Golkar district chair, although he did become a deputy area coordinator for the provincial Golkar board. The partition controversy confirmed the impression of 2005. Bachrum's local influence was becoming subordinate to the political designs of provincial and central figures.

The Mafia Defeated: The 2010 District Election

The 2010 district elections continued the pattern. In this election, the Golkar ticket defeated Bachrum's son, Andar, again demonstrating the superior influence of provincial and central politicians. Andar ran on a ticket nominated by PDI-P and a number of smaller parties, while Andar's opponents from Golkar were remarkably similar to his father's opponents in 2005. In 2005, Golkar attempted to nominate the incumbent deputy head and a provincial party functionary whose father-in-law was a senior Golkar politician. In 2010, Golkar nominated Syahrul Pasaribu, a provincial party functionary whose brother was a senior Golkar politician, and Aldinz Rafolo Siregar, the incumbent deputy head.

The Pasaribu family was one of North Sumatra's most notable political families, both during and after the New Order. The eldest brother,

Bomer, served terms in the provincial and national assemblies during the New Order, and again as a national assembly member during the post-reform era. He was the Minister of Manpower in President Gus Dur's cabinet. A second brother, Panusunan, served a term as the district head of Tapanuli Tengah during the late 1990's. When Syahrul ran for district head in Tapanuli Selatan in 2010, he was deputy chair of the Golkar provincial board and a member of the provincial assembly, where he chaired the Golkar faction. A younger brother, Gus Irawan, was director of Bank Sumut, North Sumatra's state-owned bank.

Although the brothers spent their early years in Tapanuli Selatan, they pursued their careers in Medan and beyond. Syahrul represented not Tapanuli Selatan but Simalungun district in the provincial assembly (KPU Sumut 2004). Andar's campaign attempted to portray this as a weakness and cast Andar as a local candidate more deeply attached to the district. Syahrul's campaign team, by contrast, viewed his provincial career as an asset and emphasized his connections to Medan and Jakarta. Syahrul announced his candidacy with a promise to increase "synergy" between the district,

Syahrul announced his candidacy with a promise to increase "synergy" between the district, provincial, and central governments

provincial, and central governments (*Sinar Indonesia Baru*, February 12, 2010). In the months preceding the election, Syahrul stood in for Syamsul Arifin, governor of North Sumatra and Golkar's provincial chair, at district party functions. In the days immediately preceding the election, Syahrul called in his connections. His brothers Bomer, Panusunan, and Gus Irawan came to Tapanuli Selatan to campaign on his behalf (*Metro Tabagsel*, May 8, 2010). Chairuman Harahap, one of Tapanuli Selatan's representatives to the national assembly, returned to lend support. Chaidir Ritonga, now a deputy chair of the provincial assembly, appeared in person throughout the campaign to oppose his old adversary Bachrum. Syahrul even arranged for a popular Batak singer named Eddy Silitonga to travel from Jakarta to perform at campaign events (*Metro Tabagsel*, May 9, 2010; May 7, 2010).

The machine pursued two strategies, vote-buying and identity appeals, to mobilize voters to support Syahrul. According to many accounts, vote-buying was a primary means of campaigning for many candidates, not just Syahrul. One experienced journalist, for example, estimated that 80 percent of voters chose candidates who paid them. He believed the going rate for buying votes ranged from Rp 30,000 to Rp 100,000 (US$3–US$11).[14] On the eve of the election, the vote-buying "attack at dawn" was not merely metaphorical. The director of the district development planning agency (Badan Perencana Pembangunan Daerah Tapanuli Selatan, or Bappeda) and a large group of men assaulted Hifzan Lubis, the director of the Bank Sumut branch in the neighboring district, Mandailing Natal. The assault occurred in Tapanuli Selatan at the home of Hifzan's friend and was almost certainly related to a dispute over the election. Bank Sumut, directed by Gus Irawan, was supporting Syahrul's campaign and on the night before the election it is possible that Hifzan was organizing efforts to distribute cash to buy votes. The planning agency director supported Ongku and stood to lose his job if Ongku lost. Although the papers did not report the reason for the incident, it is likely that the planning agency director resented the partisanship of Bank Sumut in general or, if it was in fact Hifzan's purpose in Tapanuli Selatan, vote-buying activities in particular (*Sinar Indonesia Baru*, May 12, 2010).

> *One journalist estimated that 80 percent of voters chose candidates who paid them*

The identity appeal that Syahrul and his running mate Aldinz made to highland residents around Sipirok town was as important as the vote-buying. Throughout the campaign period, Syahrul and Aldinz criticized Ongku for failing to transfer the seat of district government from Padang Sidempuan to Sipirok. The law partitioning the district stipulated that the move must be complete no later than 18 months after the inauguration of the new districts, but Ongku failed to meet the deadline because he lacked sufficient funds. Deputy head Aldinz, whose Siregar clan traditionally originates from Sipirok, insisted on complying and opened an office there on February 10, 2009, the last day before time expired (Nasution 2010). The tactic convinced residents that the Golkar ticket would assert Sipirok's right to seat the government and Syahrul polled over 50 percent there, winning

Tapanuli Selatan's third most populous subdistrict by a wide margin (KPU Tapsel 2010).

Syahrul decisively won the 2010 district election with 44 percent of the vote, Andar placed second with 35 percent, and Ongku finished with a mere 18 percent. Whereas in 2005 Bachrum had achieved a draw in a stand-off against senior Golkar leadership, in 2010 he was a diminished figure. During the intervening five years, Bachrum lost a high-stakes contest over partition, withdrew to Padang Lawas Utara and felt his local influence wane. Golkar meanwhile conducted highly organized district campaigns throughout North Sumatra. In 2010 party discipline was much improved and the central leadership hand-picked many of the candidates.[15]

Bachrum's decline and Golkar's return to dominance in Tapanuli Selatan was illustrated in February 2011 at the party's annual district planning meeting. Syahrul presided over the two day affair at Tapanuli Selatan's best hotel. All of Golkar's local functionaries were present, including Rahmat Nasution, Bachrum's latest successor as Golkar district chair and chair of the district assembly. Now a bit player in the party and the district, Bachrum did not attend (*Metro Tabagsel*, February 26, 2011).

Serdang Bedagai: A Machine and Mobilization

The local politics in Serdang Bedagai is an example of the Golkar machine at its best, in terms of both political dominance and administrative effectiveness. The machine, as personified by a former governor and his younger brother, used gubernatorial power to coerce the district bureaucracy, the election commission, and plantation estates to support its 2005 electoral campaign. In that election, the brothers defeated a mafia that had coalesced a few years previously when Serdang Bedagai was established as a new district. The extremely close competition between contenders, coupled with the governor's untimely death in September 2005, convinced the new district head that coercion alone would not sustain a strong administration. He undertook to mobilize a broad social coalition by offering patronage to potential allies while continuing to practice the strong-arm tactics that put him in power. The strategy successfully marginalized the former mafia and benefitted a variety of social groups, especially farmers and fisherfolk, that local government often ignores.

Of the three districts under study, Serdang Bedagai is most urban and closest to Medan. Because it is only 78 kilometers away and connected to the capital by rail as well as the Trans-Sumatra Highway, it is well integrated within provincial society. Civil servants and businessmen commute; dense networks connect NGOs and youth groups to their counterparts in Medan.

Unlike in Tapanuli Selatan and Labuhan Batu, where single economic sectors dominate, Serdang Bedagai has a relatively diversified economy. Approximately one-half of its land area is devoted to palm oil and rubber cultivation, while another quarter is rice paddy (BPS Sergai 2009, Section 5; BPS Sumut 2009, Table 5.1.3). As a result, Serdang Bedagai is one North Sumatra's leading producers of rice. Agriculture accounts for 40 percent of district GDP and manufacturing contributes another 20 percent because of local plants that process agricultural products, including palm oil, rubber, and fish. Due to the district's semi-urban character, construction, trade, services, and real estate are more profitable sectors here than in the other two districts. Nevertheless, Serdang Bedagai's economic diversity has not been able to match the growth of Labuhan Batu's boom, and per capita GDP in Serdang Bedagai remains close to the provincial median (BPS Sergai 2009, Tables 11.1, 11.3; BPS Sumut 2009, Table 11.3.3).

Serdang Bedagai was established as an independent district in 2003 when it was subdivided from Deli Serdang, surrounding the municipality of Medan. The Sultanate of Serdang, however, had a long history as a wealthy ruling house during Dutch colonial times. In 1946, when coups deposed the aristocracy throughout the province, Serdang was exceptional for its bloodless and orderly transfer of power to the Republican army (Reid 1979). The area was not so fortunate in 1965–66. Just as elsewhere in the plantation belt, suspected communists and labor activists were massacred (Tsai and Kammen 2012).

Erry Nuradi, Machine Boss

Erry Nuradi, district head of Serdang Bedagai, is widely regarded as one of the best district heads in North Sumatra, if not Indonesia. His first administration, from 2005–2010, won over 125 awards for excellence in local government, and his integrated business permits office became a model for districts throughout the country. In recognition of the district government's successful record of local development, the Ministry of Home Affairs selected Serdang Bedagai to host the Department's celebration of Regional Autonomy Day in 2009. Erry's own constituents voted overwhelmingly to reelect him in 2010, showing that they also appreciated his leadership (*Sinar Indonesia Baru*, April 24, 2010; June 14, 2010b).

Erry has been able to accomplish all of this because he benefits from local and provincial support networks. The provincial support was first, and Golkar was the focal point for these networks. His entire career Erry held positions in Golkar and affiliated organizations in Medan, where he was born, raised, and educated. A businessman, he had long held office in the Indonesian Young Businessmen's Association (Himpunan Pengusaha Muda Indonesia, HIPMI), first as general director of the Medan

> *Erry Nuradi is widely regarded as one of the best district heads in North Sumatra, if not Indonesia*

chapter, and then in the same position for the provincial organization. He had also served as the provincial deputy chair of the national youth committee (Kongres Nasional Pemuda Indonesia, KNPI), the national congress for Indonesia's youth organizations. Finally, when he was elected district head of Serdang Bedagai in 2005, Erry was serving a term as provincial secretary of Golkar, another Medan based office (KPU Sergai 2010).

Even more importantly, his older brother was governor of North Sumatra in 2005 when Erry was elected in Serdang Bedagai's first-ever district election. The governor, Rizal Nurdin, aggressively made use of his position to support Erry's candidacy. Before he retired to enter politics, Major General Rizal Nurdin had a distinguished career in the army. Rizal was selected to be governor of North Sumatra in 1998 and reelected in 2003, so on Serdang Bedagai's election day, June 27, 2005, he was midway through his second term in office.

Erry owed his local networks to Soekirman, his deputy head. Soekirman had long worked as an advocate for farmers' rights and agricultural development in a prominent North Sumatran NGO called Bitra Indonesia (Bina Keterampilan Pedesaan Indonesia [Building Rural Skills in Indonesia]). Bitra had worked extensively in Deli Serdang and Serdang Bedagai over the years and had developed a network of farmers, laborers, and activists.[16]

Once in office, Erry leveraged his party influence to build a local coalition. Patronage from the center and the province increased the amount of resources at his disposal, and he distributed it through Soekirman's networks. Erry's highly successful approach to governing Serdang Bedagai district was an example of Golkar's centralized machine expanding its reach from Indonesia's center to the districts, but it also transformed the machine into a mobilizing coalition with a wide constituent base.

The Controversial 2005 District Election

The partisanship of Governor Rizal was decisive in Serdang Bedagai's 2005 district election. Erry was a provincial politician, while his opponents, Chairullah and David Purba, were local figures ensconced in a mafia that had coalesced during the campaign to create Serdang Bedagai as a new district. They were well known and well funded. With Rizal's help Erry displaced them, winning a controversial election by a mere 954 votes. The unconvincing outcome and Rizal's death in a plane crash in September 2005 meant that Erry began his term with a weak mandate and without his most important patron.

Two years before the election, Chairullah and David Purba worked together in the campaign to separate Serdang Bedagai from the old Deli Serdang district. Chairullah publicly supported the campaign from his position as district secretary in Deli Serdang. Meanwhile, David Purba chaired the Serdang Bedagai district subdivision board (Badan Pemekaran Serdang Bedagai) and spent billions of his own rupiah supporting the campaign. He was arguably more influential than Chairullah because of his position as local leader of the youth organization Pancasila Youth (Pemuda Pancasila). In this role, David Purba directed a large network of young men who could work on construction projects, collect protection payments, and demonstrate in the streets.

After the creation of Serdang Bedagai in December 2003, Governor Rizal named Chairullah the new district's acting district head (*penjabat bupati*). The new head's tasks were to prepare the district for a direct election and to construct the offices for a new seat of local government in Sei Rampah town. He continued his working relationship with David Purba by awarding him the contract to construct the new district executive offices. By forming a coalition between the district head, a powerful business contractor, and a major youth organization, Chairullah and David Purba built Serdang Bedagai's first mafia (Hadiz 2010, 108; KPU Sergai 2010).

Though Erry Nuradi was not as well established in Serdang Bedagai as Chairullah or David Purba, he was not a newcomer to politics there. In 2004, he ran unsuccessfully for a provincial assembly seat in North Sumatra's third district, which combines Serdang Bedagai and Tebing Tinggi municipality. Soekirman had also previously tested the waters as a politician, first as an advisor to Governor Rizal and then as an unsuccessful candidate in 2004 to represent North Sumatra in the national legislature (Dewan Perwakilan Daerah, DPD) (KPU Deli Serdang 2004a; 2004b). Erry and Soekirman made a formidable ticket, but they still needed help to defeat David Purba and Chairullah. As acting district head, Chairullah had influence over the local bureaucracy and the authority to form a new election commission favorable to his candidacy. David Purba was very wealthy and had access to a local network that Soekirman would be hard pressed to match, especially in urban areas.

Erry and Soekirman's first lucky break came when Chairullah decided to run against David Purba, because the two competed for similar voters. On election day, in subdistricts where David Purba polled well, Chairullah polled poorly, and vice versa. In addition, Chairullah's decision to stand in the election gave Governor Rizal justification to remove him from his position as acting district head and to replace him with a more pliable

The commission secretary would ultimately be convicted of manipulating election returns

appointee, Kasim Siyo. Kasim Siyo's appointment was important because he, not Chairullah, appointed the staff of Serdang Bedagai's new election commission secretariat. His election secretariat supported Erry so fully that the commission secretary would ultimately be convicted of manipulating election returns and sentenced to two months in prison.

Governor Rizal intervened in other ways, too. Before the election, he called a meeting with the directors of Serdang Bedagai's plantations and asked them to support his brother Erry. His guests included managers of both private and state-owned estates. The governor wanted them to pressure their workers to vote for Erry.[17] The effort paid off on election day when two subdistricts with extensive rubber and palm oil plantations, Dolok Masihul and Dolok Merawan, returned two of Erry's best subdistrict results (KPU Sergai 2005).

Even with the governor leaning on the local bureaucracy and local businesses, the outcome of the election was extremely close. With 247,265 votes cast, Erry defeated David Purba by only 954 votes; less than one-half of one percent of the total. The tiny margin alone was cause for controversy, but in addition numerous irregularities flawed the election and prompted David Purba's supporters to accuse Governor Rizal, the election commission, and Erry of election fraud (*Suara Karya Online*, September 29, 2005).

The headline of North Sumatra's *Waspada* daily two days after the province-wide round of elections read "Binjai and Serdang Bedagai Elections Flawed" (*Waspada*, June 29, 2005b). The newspaper criticized the Serdang Bedagai election commission because it delayed the release of tabulation data and at the time the edition went to press the commission still had not made any announcements regarding the outcome. It further reported that confusion over collecting ballots had triggered rumors that the election commission was manipulating data.

Besides *Waspada*, the official election monitoring committee (*panwaslu*) also suspected fraud. In a letter to the election commission, it recommended that six villages repeat the polling because of evidence that ballot-stuffing affected the results in those villages. For his part, David Purba appealed the outcome of the election to the state high court in Medan (Pengadilan Tinggi).

Whatever the merits of David Purba's appeal, the provincial and central levels of government endorsed Erry's victory. On July 25, 2005, the state high court in Medan overruled David Purba's appeal and confirmed Erry's victory. Shortly after that, the Ministry of Home Affairs issued a letter formally recognizing the election result (*Suara Karya Online*, September 29, 2005).

Official recognition could not quiet the protests, however, especially when in August the secretary of the election commission, Lilik, was convicted of manipulating election data and sentenced to two months in prison. Despite the embarrassment of the conviction and the objections of the protesters demonstrating in front of the Ministry of Home Affairs, the state high court refused to reconsider its ruling and Erry began his first term as district head of Serdang Bedagai (*Suara Karya Online*, August 30, 2005).

To achieve victory in 2005, Erry exploited his connections at the provincial level to win at the district level. Governor Rizal ensured that the local bureaucratic administration was supportive of his brother's candidacy; he pressured local plantation businesses to get their employees out to vote, and in all likelihood he authorized election fraud. But on September 6, 2005, Rizal Nurdin died in an airplane crash on his way to a meeting in Jakarta with the president and Indonesia's other governors. The governor's death deprived Erry of his most important patron at a time when he was embroiled in controversy. Although the election had been decided, David Purba would continue to be a formidable opponent that Erry would have to face without the backing of his powerful brother.

> *To achieve victory in 2005, Erry exploited his connections at the provincial level to win at the district level*

From Provincial Backing to a Local Coalition

Though Erry began as an outsider to Serdang Bedagai, he systematically constructed a broad local coalition during his time in office so that he no longer required outside help when he ran for reelection in 2010. His local support was so unchallenged in 2010 that Erry won by the widest margin of any of North Sumatra's 20 district elections. Erry and Soekirman won 56 percent of the vote and defeated Chairullah's and David Purba's combined ticket by a margin of 30 percent (KPU Sumut 2010a).

Erry constructed the local coalition in three ways. He cultivated influential allies from four different social categories: business, farmers, the press, and NGOs; he consolidated his influence over four formal institutions of the state predisposed to support him: the bureaucracy, the election commission, Golkar, and the district assembly; and he attacked his opponents (namely David Purba, Chairullah, and an activist named Jhonni Sitompul) with legal prosecution and bureaucratic reassignments. In pursuing these tactics, Erry deployed his influence at the provincial and central levels of government to obtain extra resources and leverage, but he also leaned heavily on the local connections of his deputy Soekirman.

Reaching out to potential allies

Erry's administration endeared itself to business in two ways. First, it enacted policies that reduced bureaucratic red tape for business and avoided gratuitous local taxes and fees. In 2006, Erry established North Sumatra's first integrated business permits office to streamline the regulatory process in the district. The program gained national attention for its progress toward making business regulation more efficient, transparent, and accountable (YIPD 2009).

Second, Erry's approach to tendering projects materially benefited local business. Erry preferred to tender many small projects as opposed to a few large, high-prestige projects.[18] During his first term, for example, Erry constructed 29 new schools, including 11 high schools, throughout Serdang Bedagai. He built 76 new health clinics of varying sizes (*Bulletin Serdang Bedagai* 2010a; 2010b). With the exception of a new hospital and a new district assembly building, the high schools were Erry's most high-value tenders. The model

> *Erry was able to direct projects to his favorite contractors and still tender enough contracts to keep everyone else in business too*

meant that Erry tendered a large number of projects with short completion times and budget allocations turned over to new projects every year. In other words, local businesses benefited from frequent opportunities to win government tenders. As a result, few local businessmen criticized Erry's administration, publicly or privately. Erry was able to direct projects to his favorite contractors, one of whom was his brother-in-law, Azmi Yuli Sitorus, and still tender enough contracts to keep everyone else in business too.

Erry's first administration reached out to peasant farmers through deputy head Soekirman's local connections and Erry's provincial and national ones. While in office, Soekirman repeatedly met with farmers. In 2006, for example, he received a delegation of 1,000 farmers and agreed in principle with their opposition to imported rice. In 2008, he delivered the opening address at the inaugural congress of the Serdang Bedagai peasant farmers' association (Serikat Petani Serdang Bedagai) (Khairul 2006; Bitra Indonesia, July 5, 2009). Erry used his influence with the provincial and central government to procure extra assistance for Serdang Bedagai's farmers and fisherman. In 2008, the district received provincial earmarks to stabilize the price of corn and to establish a pilot program for green mussel farming. In 2009, the central Department of Ocean Fisheries (Departemen Kelautan dan Perikanan) selected Serdang Bedagai as a recipient of special funds to support fishing cooperatives (*Sinar Indonesia Baru*, 17 December 2008; *Analisa Daily*, 4 December 2008; 15 January 2009). Erry's influence also helped the district promote these efforts. In 2008 and 2009, the president of Indonesia named Serdang Bedagai the winner of consecutive food production awards, honors about which the district government tirelessly reminded voters (*Bulletin Serdang Bedagai* 2009c).

The signature farming project of Erry's first term began before Serdang Bedagai existed as a district, but that has not discouraged Erry from taking credit for it. In 2003, the Indonesian Ministry of Public Works began rehabilitating the Ular River irrigation system with funding provided by a loan from the Japanese International Cooperation Agency. The project was nearing completion in 2010, and the district administration boasted to voters that it would provide irrigation to 18,500 hectares of rice paddy (Bappenas 2010).

For those villagers unconvinced by the administration's various farm-friendly projects, Erry offered a more tangible sign of support in the year preceding the election. In 2009, Erry rewarded every village chief in Serdang Bedagai with an official motorbike for conducting village business (*Bulletin Serdang Bedagai* 2009a). No doubt Erry hoped that these influential community leaders would remember the gifts during the 2010 election campaign.

Finally, Erry cultivated alliances with influential activists in NGOs and the local press. Soekirman was the bridge to the NGO community. In 2006 the administration solicited input from Soekirman's former organization, Bitra, when it was developing the integrated business permits office. Soekirman frequently made public appearances with NGO activists. During the festivities to mark World Food Day 2010, for example, Soekirman participated in a public dialogue with a district assembly member, the director of Bitra, and the chair of a state-sponsored farmers' association (Gabungan Kelompok Tani, or Gapoktan) (*Berita Sore*, October 26, 2010).

Erry's administration reached out to journalists primarily through its public relations division (Bagian Hubungan Masyarakat). The office hosted journalists at the executive offices and distributed high quality press releases that made their jobs much easier. Many of these releases appeared verbatim in local newspapers. On occasion, Erry personally met journalists and asked them to temper criticism. He did this on several occasions with Jhonni Sitompul, who wrote for a major Medan daily and was one of Erry's most outspoken critics.[19]

Consolidating control over state institutions

While Erry courted allies in society, he tightened his grip on Serdang Bedagai's formal state institutions: the bureaucracy, the election commission, political parties, and the district assembly. As a result of Governor Rizal's intervention, Erry began his administration with the bureaucracy and election commission already sympathetic to him. Erry carefully nurtured this partisanship. He made bureaucratic appointments based on personal loyalty and brought much of his staff with him from Medan (*Waspada Online*, July 14, 2009). Erry showed how highly he valued loyalty with his first appointment to district secretary, the district's top bureaucrat. Many local observers expected him to reward Aliman Siregar, an important campaign supporter in 2005, with an appointment as district secretary. It was rumored that the two had made a quid pro quo agreement to exchange support for the appointment. When he made the selection, however, Erry passed over Aliman in favor of Nasrun Husin Lubis.[20]

In his efforts to maintain the favor of the election commission, Erry made a rare miscalculation. He provoked outrage during the fasting month in 2009 when he paid for three commission members to take the *umroh* pilgrimage to Mecca. The resulting scandal cost two of Erry's allies in the commission their jobs, but a third Erry ally ultimately became the new commission chairperson. While the commissioners were still abroad, the local press picked up the story, and the national press quickly followed suit. The provincial election commission denounced the gift and reported it to the ethics council (Dewan Kehormatan). The resulting scrutiny revealed further irregularities, and two of the pilgrims plus one other commission member were ultimately sacked for accepting bribes during the 2009 general elections (*Kompas*, November 10, 2009). The ethics council also recommended that the third pilgrim, Syarianto, be removed from the commission for accepting Erry's gift. Syarianto nevertheless retained his position because he was not implicated for taking bribes (*Kompas*, November 27, 2009). In the reorganized election commission, the five members elected Syarianto as the new commission chair, and Erry's links to the commission weathered the scandal damaged but intact.

Unlike many other district heads, Erry never faced a hostile district assembly. During 2004 to 2009, Golkar controlled 10 seats in the assembly, one more than rival PDI-P. The remaining 26 seats were divided among 12 other parties (BPS Sergai 2006, Table 2.2.1). M. Yusuf Basrun chaired both the local Golkar chapter and the assembly, while Erry maintained a leadership position within the party as regional coordinator for the provincial board (Ketua Koordinator Daerah II). Erry thus indirectly supervised the largest faction in the assembly. When Basrun's term as district party chair ended in 2010, Erry succeeded him, further solidifying his grip on Golkar locally (*Waspada*, 17 February 2010). After the 2009 general elections, Erry's dominance over the district assembly became even more pronounced. Two of Erry's closest cronies won assembly seats representing two different parties. Azmi Yuli Sitorus, Erry's brother-in-law, became the chair of the Democrat Party faction which controlled seven seats, while Usman Sitorus chaired the PPP faction and five seats. Between Golkar, with six seats, Democrat and PPP, Erry controlled 40 percent of the seats in the district assembly (*Bulletin Serdang Bedagai* 2009b).

Attacking opponents

Erry harassed political opponents as skillfully as he built alliances and manipulated political organizations. Erry typically pursued two lines of attack: he undermined rivals' livelihoods and he brought them to court. In both respects he frequently exercised his provincial and central influence. During his first term in Serdang Bedagai, Erry used this one-two combination against David Purba, Chairullah, and Jhonni Sitompul.

David Purba was Erry's most threatening rival because he controlled Pemuda Pancasila. In 2008, Erry became a member of the advisory council to the North Sumatra provincial leadership of Pemuda Pancasila. The same year, after 20 years of holding office in Pemuda Pancasila, David Purba failed to win reelection as the chair of the Serdang Bedagai chapter of the organization. In 2010, when David Purba again ran for political office in Serdang Bedagai, he was no longer affiliated with Pemuda Pancasila but had struck up an unlikely alliance with the traditionalist Islamic organization, Nadhlatul Ulama.

Just as he interfered in David Purba's career, Erry attacked the livelihoods of Chairullah and Jhonni Sitompul. For six years after Governor Rizal sacked him, Chairullah languished at the provincial board for national unity and community protection (Badan Kesatuan Bangsa dan Perlindungan Masyarakat). In 2010, Erry reassigned Jhonni Sitompul's wife to a health clinic in the remote subdistrict Silinda after she had worked for years in the important district town of Pasar Bengkel. Her position had included an official house as a perquisite, so Jhonni's family lost their home as a result of the reassignment.

In the case of each of these three political opponents, Erry brought them to court in addition to attacking their livelihoods. In 2004, while Chairullah was still acting district head in Serdang Bedagai, the provincial prosecutor initiated a corruption investigation against him for crimes he allegedly committed while still district secretary of Deli Serdang (Batubara and Bambang 2004). After Governor Rizal's death, the investigation steadily proceeded and in 2007 the state court in Lubukpakam, Deli Serdang, convicted Chairullah of corruption and sentenced him to eighteen months imprisonment. The following year, the North Sumatra high court upheld the decision and added six months to the sentence. Chairullah again appealed the decision, but in August 2010 the Supreme Court upheld the high court's decision (*Pos Metro Medan*, January 14, 2011). In addition to this long-running case, in March 2010 a central anticorruption commission (KPK) investigation team questioned the beleaguered Chairullah about his actions as acting district head of Serdang Bedagai. The investigation, which took place only

> *In the case of each of [his] three political opponents, Erry brought them to court in addition to attacking their livelihoods*

two months before the district election, targeted both Chairullah and David Purba because of a reforestation tender Chairullah's administration awarded to David Purba in 2005 (*Sumut Pos*, March 26, 2010).

In September 2009, the Medan police arrested David Purba on charges of fraud valued at 200 million rupiah, or US$20,000. The prosecution witness was a business associate of David's who had lent him the money in 2007. The project for which David borrowed the money fell through, and he never returned the money. The case was tried in the Medan state court in June 2010, just a month after the election, and David Purba was eventually sentenced to six months in prison and twelve months probation (*Waspada Online*, March 3, 2010). Rumors in Serdang Bedagai allege that someone, presumably associated with Erry, offered to pay the witness an amount equal to David's debt if he agreed to testify against David in court.[21]

Jhonni Sitompul was involved in an altercation with two security guards at the district revenue office (Pendapatan Pengelolaan Keuangan dan Asset Daerah) in August 2009. Both sides accused the other of assault and reported the incident to the local police, and both cases were tried in the Tebing Tinggi state court in February 2010. Jhonni was sentenced to probation, while the security guards were sentenced to four and eight months in prison (*Pos Metro Medan*, February 25, 2010).

It is unlikely that three of Erry's most important opponents all faced legal prosecution during the 2010 campaign period by coincidence. Erry made the most of his opponents' indiscretions and prosecuted them when the opportunity arose. These three cases demonstrate the impressive reach of Erry's influence within the justice system. Chairullah's case originated in the Lubukpakam state court and the appeals process reached the Supreme Court. David Purba was tried in the Medan state court, and Jhonni Sitompul in the Tebing Tinggi state court. Different public prosecutors handled each case. Even the KPK visited from Jakarta to investigate both of Erry's electoral opponents just two months before the district election. Regardless of the prosecutor and venue, each case returned a conviction of Erry's opponents, excepting only the KPK's preliminary investigation.

During his first term in office, Erry constructed a broad local coalition of support that included local business, farmers, NGO activists, the bureaucracy, the election commission, the district assembly, and parts of the youth groups. He undermined the livelihoods and secured criminal convictions of his chief rivals. He accomplished these things by utilizing party and personal networks to direct patronage to his allies and to apply coercive pressure to his opponents. Erry used money politics and dirty tricks as well as any of his competitors, but he also distributed benefits broadly to groups of supporters, particularly rural farmers and the business community. He chose coalition-building strategies that shared patronage so widely that in some instances it began to approximate a public good, such as with the building of schools and health clinics. Thus, even as Erry entrenched a party machine in Serdang Bedagai, he experimented with more pluralistic politics. By the 2010 election, Erry had created a mobilizing coalition.

Conclusion: Political Mafias and a Party Machine in North Sumatra

This study argues that at least three types of coalitions contend for power at the district level in Indonesia. These coalitions amass political strength from the institutional resource base at their disposal. Different institutions provide different resources, with the result that not all coalitions have the same "menu" of strategic options. In Labuhan Batu, Tapanuli Selatan, and Serdang Bedagai districts, the most consequential institutions were (1) the local state apparatus, (2) party organizations

> *Not all coalitions have the same "menu" of strategic options*

which have the ability to override the provincial bureaucracy, and (3) social networks with the potential to mobilize popular constituencies. In those districts, political mafias dependent on the local state alone contended against a Golkar machine which bridged district and provincial governments. In some cases, popular constituencies contributed decisive support to either mafias or machines when they were incorporated into mobilizing coalitions. These contests featured money, coercion, and popular mobilization to the degree that each coalition could summon such resources.

How representative of the rest of Indonesia is this pattern of contention among coalitions? This paper hypothesizes that similar elite coalitions will coalesce in other districts to the extent that similar resources—namely local state spoils, party influence, and strong social networks—are available to elites. It asserts that this is most likely to be the case in Outer Island districts that neither benefit from significant oil, gas, or mineral revenues nor enjoy special autonomous status. While a full survey of Indonesia's districts is beyond the scope of this study, this conclusion situates the three case studies within the larger field of cases in North Sumatra, where 20 districts (excluding those on Nias Island) conducted local elections in 2010 and 2011. In doing so, it assesses the plausibility of the hypothesis given the outcomes of these elections.

The 2010 Local Elections in North Sumatra

Within North Sumatra, mafias and machines are discernable in many, though not all, districts and broadly conform to the following geographic pattern of distribution: a Golkar machine predominated on the coasts, incumbent mafias were most successful in the highland interior, and palm oil–funded challengers captured office in booming plantation districts. Mobilizing coalitions are more difficult to detect on the basis of a brief survey of election results, but plantation districts are likely candidates. An overview of the North Sumatra 2010 local elections is presented in the appendix.

Golkar has successfully established a machine in North Sumatra, while PDI-P and Democrat Party have not, primarily because Golkar controls the governor's office. Gubernatorial power over the provincial bureaucracy confers access to patronage and allows Golkar to appoint loyalists to strategic positions, especially in new districts. In addition, over the last three legislative elections, Golkar has maintained a consistent district and provincial legislative presence while PDI-P's and Democrat's legislative shares have ebbed and flowed. Finally, Golkar's central board campaigned aggressively on behalf of its local candidates in 2010. In other provinces, Golkar may not enjoy such a privileged position. PDI-P, Democrat, or any other party might build a rival machine if it can link local and provincial institutions as Golkar has done in North Sumatra.

In both the eastern and western coastal lowlands of North Sumatra, Golkar candidates replaced mafias that had held power for two terms. The outgoing incumbents, precluded from running for office by the two-term limit, advanced proxy candidates to succeed them in three districts and four cities. Only two proxies were elected, however, suggesting the instability of local mafias. Instead, Golkar's machine dominated. Party-supported candidates took office in three districts and two cities, including Medan, Asahan, and Serdang Bedagai, three of the four most populous jurisdictions conducting elections. (The second most populous district to conduct an election in 2010 was Simalungun.)

In the highlands, mafias outperformed Golkar but both did badly. Three incumbent mafias in Humbang Hasundutan, Samosir, and Pakpak Bharat were reelected in campaigns marred by violence. In four other interior districts incumbent candidates lost reelection campaigns, once again underscoring mafia instability. Golkar fared even worse, supporting only two winning candidates.

In elections where incumbents and Golkar both lost, many palm oil candidates won. The sons of plantation tycoons won in Mandailing Natal district and Pematang Siantar municipality, and in all three Labuhan Batu districts the winning candidates campaigned with the financial backing of palm oil planters. The campaigns of aspiring palm oil mafias involved varying degrees of organization. In all likelihood they bought many votes, but some, such as in Labuhan Batu, also mobilized popular constituencies.

What explains geographic variation within North Sumatra among the types of dominant elite coalitions? While a complete explanation would require further research, the analysis presented in this study suggests a few hypotheses. In accordance with the argument that party machines possess institutional advantages over political mafias, a machine dominated North Sumatra's most populous and strategic bailiwicks. A combination of judicial prosecutions, vote buying, patronage, and popular mobilizing swept Golkar candidates to victory in nearly every district and city around Medan. These districts command North Sumatra's economy and will have the greatest impact on the 2014 general elections. In the sparsely populated highlands, Golkar may simply have had less interest in campaigning. It may also be the case, however, that the patronage resource pressures that bedevil mafias elsewhere are less severe in these districts, making mafias more competitive. In plantation districts, finally, aspiring mafias enjoy the benefits of global demand for palm oil. Windfall profits have made local plantation owners uniquely influential and tipped the balance of power in favor of palm oil–led coalitions.

The pattern of variation is invisible without first disaggregating the category of "New Order elites." Suharto's regime so encompassed

Indonesia's political, economic, and social life that it is natural that many post-reform elites would be its heirs, save those whom the regime excluded from power, such as traditional ethnic leaders. Accordingly, the variation documented in this study is consistent with the work that demonstrates continuity between the New Order and post-reform eras. However, emphasizing continuity risks overlooking the considerable variation in and between the types of coalitions that are engaged in local politics.

Similarly, studies of "money politics" that do not consider the institutional sources of patronage or the coalitional relationships that develop around it create a mistaken impression of uniformity. Though political mafias, party machines, and mobilizing coalitions all distribute patronage, they extract it from different resource bases and employ it according to different orientations. The following sections discuss the implications of these differences for policy decisions and electoral competition.

Countering Decentralization Reform

Viewed from a purely local perspective, it appears that political mafias must expand or perish. The potential of the local state apparatus as a resource base is too limited to satisfy both the expectations of coalition members and the demands of election campaigning. In the 2010 elections, incumbents performed dismally when they limited their coalitions to

> *Viewed from a purely local perspective, it appears that political mafias must expand or perish.*

bureaucratic officials, assembly members, and business contractors—that is, strictly to the members of a local mafia. The most successful mafias expanded their coalitions by mobilizing popular constituencies or by accommodating machines.

Factors beyond the district, however, may prevent mafias from expanding. In particular, central efforts to curtail what have been depicted as the excessive dangers of decentralization are increasingly undermining the ability of mafias to generate patronage. As early as 2002, the Megawati administration was pursuing legislation intended to reestablish central authority to manage natural resources and to sanction district governments. President Megawati's counterreforms culminated with Law No. 32/2004 on regional government, which she signed just before leaving office. By creating direct local elections and requiring party nominations that represent 15 percent of the electorate, the law inflated campaign costs and placed new strains on political mafias. In addition, it took several initial steps toward making districts subservient once again to provinces and the center (Buehler 2010).

The Yudhoyono administration extended Megawati's recentralization agenda. Law No. 28/2009, for example, established a closed-list of allowable local taxes. In 2010 the administration was considering a radical revision to Law No. 32/2004 that would give governors extensive powers over the districts, including sole responsibility to appoint, promote, and reassign local civil servants (Effendi and Sony 2011).

The new legislation, combined with the shortcomings of mafias, created the opportunity for national parties to step in to local government, replacing mafias. In North Sumatra, Golkar is the party which has done the most to take advantage, and its candidates have replaced local mafias in at least seven North Sumatran districts and cities since 2005 (see appendix). Less than ten years after reforms took effect, counterreform has restored the advantage to centralized parties in contests over control of the regions, at least in North Sumatra.

Golkar candidates have replaced local mafias in at least seven North Sumatran districts and cities since 2005

Two issues particularly important to local politicians in North Sumatra, plantation revenue sharing and forest reclassification, illustrate the stakes of recentralization. Since the 1990s, successive governors have lobbied the central government to return a share of the vast plantation revenues generated in North Sumatra to the province. It is not surprising that during the New Order the plea was ignored. But in 2006, sixteen governors of plantation-rich provinces signed a letter to the president requesting 25 percent ownership of the state-owned estates and an 80 percent share of the export taxes levied on their products (*Suara Pembaruan*, May 12, 2006). Despite initially promising to act on the request, to date President Yudhoyono has not, preferring instead to maintain central control over the lucrative revenues. North Sumatra has been similarly helpless promoting provincial forest reclassification. In 2005, the Ministry of Forestry issued a decree letter (SK Menhut No. 44/2005) fixing the province's forest boundaries at 3,742,120 hectares, classified into various categories. The letter elicited widespread consternation because government offices and villages alike fell within forest boundaries, losing their legal standing (Munthe 2007). The affected districts, in coordination with the provincial government, proposed boundary revisions intended to drastically reduce forest reserves, presumably in order to maximize logging opportunities and to mask illegally logged areas. In 2009 the governor submitted a revised and weakened proposal to the ministry, but the central government, emboldened by North Sumatra's internal bickering, dragged its feet (*Kompas*, November 18, 2009). On both of these important issues, the central government has maintained a strong enough position vis-à-vis the regions to dictate the timing and terms of the debate.

Competitive Elections
Paradoxically, counterreform made the 2010 local elections in North Sumatra more competitive than the previous round. Only seven incumbents or proxies won reelection in 2010, compared to ten in 2005. Competition increased after recentralizing legislation empowered party machines to displace established mafias in many districts. As a result, the most consequential contests occurred vertically, between locally oriented mafias and centrally oriented machines, not horizontally, between rival factions.

The heightened competition increased democratic participation in two ways. First, elections presented a meaningful choice to voters, as the difference in orientation between political mafias and party machines affects the local government's capacity to distribute patronage as well as its attitude toward issues such as plantation revenue sharing and forest reclassification. Voters were able to sanction unpopular incumbents and North Sumatrans did not hesitate to do so by rejecting many incumbent candidates and their proxies. Second, close competition among contending candidates pressured some to reach out to new constituencies in an effort to attract more votes. Some mafias and machines expanded their coalitions in some places to include NGOs, youth groups, farmers' associations, local communities, and religious associations. Once they join a coalition, social organizations expect elites to respond to their concerns and distribute patronage to their members. In this way, they involve their constituencies in the political process and may, through the threat of withdrawing their support, help to hold local governments accountable.

If Golkar's machine continues to dominate local politics in North Sumatra, however, intense electoral competition may well prove to have been temporary. The year 2010 may signal a shift away from mafias and toward machines. Palm oil mafias, confined to plantation districts and dependent on volatile commodity markets, pose a contingent, localized threat to Golkar but do not challenge its overall predominance. If other local mafias continue to decline, and current national policy trends suggest that they might, then viable challengers may not emerge in 2015 to oppose the provincial machine's incumbents. Under such circumstances, high levels of participation are unlikely to reoccur. As Steven Erie (1988) argues of urban machines in the United States, once they consolidate control over a city, machines limit access to the patronage rolls. Absent the threat of losing power, machines have every incentive to expend patronage only to reward tenured members of the coalition.

It is difficult to make generalizations about Indonesia's democracy, even those limited in scope to North Sumatra, because it continues to change very rapidly. Each round of local elections has favored different elites and produced different types of governments. Nevertheless, some questions appear settled, at least temporarily. Local government in North Sumatra has not been taken over by dynastic bosses in the manner of the Philippines. The 2010 elections, in contrast to the Philippines, demonstrated the deficiencies of the local state as a source of dynastic political power. Instead, party machines relied on provincial power and patronage to seize office in strategic local jurisdictions, even without previously existing grassroots support. As a result, local government in North Sumatra, at least for the next several years, will be dominated by the concerns of a machine as Golkar prepares for the 2014 general elections.

Appendix:
Overview of the 2010 North Sumatra Elections[1]

	Location	Golkar Wins	Incumbent Wins	Incumbent Loses	Interpretation
East Coast	Medan City	Yes	Yes		Machine
	Serdang Bedagai	Yes	Yes		Machine → Mobilization
	Asahan	Yes	No	Proxy incumbent	Machine
	Tanjung Balai City[2]	Yes	No	Proxy incumbent	Machine
	Tebing Tinggi City[3]	No	Yes (Proxy)		Mafia
	Labuhan Batu	No	No	Proxy incumbent	Mafia → Mobilization
	Labuhan Batu Utara	No	No		Palm oil mafia
	Labuhan Batu Selatan	No	No		Palm oil mafia
	Binjai City	No	No	Proxy incumbent	?

	Location	Golkar Wins	Incumbent Wins	Incumbent Loses	Interpretation
Interior Highlands	Tapanuli Selatan	Yes	No	Incumbent	Machine
	Pakpak Bharat	Yes	No[4]	Proxy incumbent	Mafia
	Samosir	No	Yes	Deputy incumbent	Mafia
	Humbang Hasundutan	No	Yes		Mafia
	Pematang Siantar City	No	No	Incumbent	Palm oil mafia
	Simalungun	No	No	Incumbent	?
	Toba Samosir	No	No	Incumbent	?
	Karo	No	No		?
West Coast	Tapanuli Tengah[5]	Yes	No	Proxy incumbent	Machine
	Sibolga City	No[6]	Yes (Proxy)	Deputy incumbent	Mafia
	Mandailing Natal	No	No		Palm oil mafia

1. Chart compiled from various sources.

2. On September 28, 2010, the Constitutional Court (Mahkamah Konstitusi) ordered Tanjung Balai to repeat the election in 17 wards because of "systematic money politics." Golkar's candidate won the follow-up election.

3. On June 9, 2010, the Constitutional Court ruled the victorious Golkar candidate ineligible because he was under probation for a previous corruption conviction. The incumbent's younger brother won the follow-up election.

4. Although technically not the incumbent, the victorious candidate was incumbent deputy executive and the younger brother of the 2005 election winner, who had died in office.

5. The Tapanuli Tengah election took place on March 12, 2011.

6. Although the candidate that Golkar nominated lost, the candidate who won was previously a Golkar representative in the national assembly.

Endnotes

1. At the local level, Indonesia is administratively divided into rural districts (*kabupaten*) and urban municipalities (*kota*). For simplicity, the study will often use the term "district" to refer collectively to *kabupaten* and *kota*. Similarly, "district head" will refer to executives in both *kabupaten* (*bupati*) and *kota* (*walikota*).

2. The reforms were initially formulated in Laws No. 22/1999 and No. 25/1999, later revised in Laws No. 32/2004 and 33/2004.

3. Indirect elections were provided for in Laws No. 2/1999, No. 3/1999 and No. 4/1999; Law No. 32/2004 revised the election procedures.

4. *Pemekaran wilayah* is the Indonesian term for forming new districts by subdividing existing ones.

5. In contrast to Indonesia's locally circumscribed political mafias, however, *chao pho* "godfathers" in Thailand have successfully extended their influence to national politics.

6. The one exception was during 2005–2008, when Rudolf Pardede of PDI-P succeeded Rizal Nurdin after the latter died in office.

7. Personal interview, technician, Rantauprapat, August 31, 2010.

8. Personal interview, journalist, Rantauprapat, August 31, 2010.

9. Personal interview, former assembly member, Rantauprapat, September 7, 2010.

10. Personal interview, campaign organizer, Rantauprapat, June 17, 2010.

11. Ibid.

12. Personal interview, former assembly member, Rantauprapat, September 7, 2010.

13. Personal interview, campaign organizer, Rantauprapat, June 17, 2010.

14. Personal interview, journalist, Padang Sidempuan, May 11, 2010.

15. Personal interview, activist, Medan, September 22, 2010.

16. Personal interview, activist, Perbaungan, September 29, 2010.

17. Personal interview, activist, Medan, March 25, 2011.

18. Personal interview, journalist, Tebing Tinggi, October 11, 2010.

19. Personal interview, journalist, Tebing Tinggi, March 26, 2011.

20. Personal interview, journalist, Tebing Tinggi, October 11, 2010.

21. Ibid.

Bibliography

Analisa Daily. 2008. "Sergai Bakal Jadi 'Pilot Project' Pengembangan Budidaya Kerang Hijau di Sumut," December 4.

———. 2009. "Departemen Kelautan dan Perikanan Kucurkan Dana Rp 2 Miliar untuk Sergai," January 15.

Aspinall, Edward, Sebastian Dettman, and Eve Warburton. 2011. "When Religion Trumps Ethnicity: A Regional Election Case Study from Indonesia." *South East Asia Research* 19.1: 27–58.

Bappenas (Badan Perencanaan dan Pembangunan Nasional). 2010. "Permasalahan Proyek-proyek Pinjaman JICA Tahun Anggaran 2010, Posisi: 31 Maret 2010," March 31. Accessed April 15, 2011, www.bappenas.go.id/get-file-server /node/9968/.

Barter, Shane. 2008. "The Dangers of Decentralization: Clientelism, the State, & Nature in a Democratic Indonesia." *Federal Governance* 1:6: 1–15.

Baskoro, L.R., Danto, Agung Wijaya, and Hambali Batubara. 2006. "Penjarahan Kayu: Sewindu untuk Sang Penantang," *Majalah Tempo*, August 7.

Batubara, Hambali and Bambang Soed. 2004. "Bupati Serdang Tersangka Korupsi," *Tempo Interaktif*, December 15. www.tempointeraktif.com.

Batubara, Yos. 2009. "Evaluasi Hasi Penyelenggaraan Pemilu 2009: Dari Babak Baru Pemilihan Secara Langsung Tahun 2004 Ke Babak Pemilihan Secara Langsung Dengan Suara Terbanyak Tahun 2009 Kabupaten Labuhanbatu—Sumatera Utara." *TePI Indonesia*.

Berita Sore. 2010. "Hari Pangan Sedunia 2010 Sumut Di Sergai," October 26. www. beritasore.com.

Bitra Indonesia. 2009. "Petani Sergai Laksanakan Kongres Pertama," July 5. Accessed April 8, 2011, bitra.or.id.

BPS Sergai (Badan Pusat Statistik Serdang Bedagai). 2006. "Kabupaten Serdang Bedagai in Figures 2006."

_____. 2009. "Kabupaten Serdang Bedagai in Figures 2009."

BPS Sumut (Badan Pusat Statistik Sumatera Utara). 2009. "Sumatera Utara in Figures 2009."

Buehler, Michael. 2009. "The Rising Importance of Personal Networks in Indonesian Local Politics: An Analysis of District Government Head Elections in South Sulawesi in 2005." In *Deepening Democracy in Indonesia? Direct Elections for Local Leaders (Pilkada),* edited by Maribeth Erb and Priyambudi Sulistiyanto, 101–124. Singapore: ISEAS.

_____. 2010. "Decentralisation and Local Democracy in Indonesia: The Marginalisation of the Public Sphere." In *Problems of Democratisation in Indonesia: Elections, Institutions and Society,* edited by Edward Aspinall and Marcus Mietzner, 267–285. Singapore: ISEAS.

Buehler, Michael and Paige Tan. 2007. "Party Candidate Relationships in Indonesian Local Politics: A Case Study of the 2005 Regional Elections in Gowa, South Sulawesi Province." *Indonesia* 84: 41–69.

Bulletin Serdang Bedagai. 2009a. "Seluruh Kepdes Sergai Dapat Kendaraan Operasional," Edition XX July–August.

_____. 2009b. "Keputusan Gubernur Sumatera Utara No: 170/4087.K/Tahun 2009, Tanggal 12 Oktober 2009: Pengangkatan Anggota DPRD Kabupaten Sergai Periode 2009 – 2014," Edition XXI September–October.

_____. 2009c. "2 Kali Berturut-turut: Sergai Terima Penghargaan Ketapang, Tingkat Nasional & Provinsi," Edition XXII November–December.

_____. 2010a. "H.T. Nuradi & H. Soekirman: 5 Tahun Sukses Memimpin Sergai," Special Edition XXVI July–August.

_____. 2010b. "Sehat, Modal Dasar Pembangunan," Special Edition XXVI July–August.

Collier, David and James Mahoney. 1996. "Insights and Pitfalls: Selection Bias in Qualitative Research." *World Politics* 49.1: 56–91.

Davidson, Jamie. 2007. "Politics-As-Usual On Trial: Regional Anti-corruption Campaigns in Indonesia." *The Pacific Review* 20.1: 75–99.

_____. 2009. "Studies of Massive, Collective Violence in Post-Soeharto Indonesia." *Critical Asian Studies* 41.2: 329–349.

Davidson, Jamie and David Henley, eds. 2007. *The Revival of Tradition in Indonesian Politics: The Deployment of Adat from Colonialism to Indigenism.* New York: Routledge.

Disbun Sumut (Dinas Perkebunan Propinsi Sumatera Utara). 2004a. "Rekapitulasi Luas Areal dan Produksi Komoditi Kelapa Sawit Propinsi Sumatera Utar. Accessed April 15, 2010, www.deptan.go.id/daerah_new/sumut/disbun _sumut/index.

_____. 2004b. "Rekapitulasi Luas Areal dan Produksi Komoditi Karet per Kabupaten di Propinsi Sumatera Utara." Accessed April 15, 2010, www.deptan.go.id /daerah_new/sumut/disbun_sumut/index.

DPK (Direktorat Jenderal Perimbangan Keuangan). 2010. "Data APBD Tahun 2010," *Kementerian Keuangan Republik Indonesia*, July 20. Accessed June 23, 2011, www.djpk.depkeu.go.id.

Economist. 2011. "Power to the People! No, Wait…" March 19.

Effendi, Cecep and Sony Sjahril. 2011. "Reshaping Regional Autonomy," *Jakarta Post*, February 14.

Erie, Steven. 1988. *Rainbow's End: Irish-Americans and the Dilemma of Urban Machine Politics, 1840–1985.* Berkeley: University of California Press.

Ford, Michele. 2009. *Workers and Intellectuals: NGOs, Trade Unions and the Indonesian Labour Movement.* Honolulu: University of Hawai'i Press.

Hadi Shubhan, M. 2006. "'Recall': Antara Hak Partai Politik dan Hak Berpolitik Anggota Parpol." *Jurnal Konstitusi* 3.4: 30–57.

Hadiz, Vedi. 2003. "Power and Politics in North Sumatra: The Uncompleted *Reformasi.*" In *Local Power and Politics in Indonesia: Decentralisation & Democratisation*, edited by Edward Aspinall and Greg Fealy, 119–131. Singapore: ISEAS.

_____. 2010. *Localising Power in Post-Authoritarian Indonesia: A Southeast Asia Perspective.* Stanford: Stanford University Press.

Harahap, Fajar Dame. 2008. "KPK Prioritaskan Korupsi di Labuhanbatu," *Medan Bisnis,* December 2.

_____. 2009. "GOR Rantauprapat Terbesar di Sumut Diresmikan," *Ekspos News*, November 19. eksposnews.com.

Hasugian, Maria and Hambali Batubara. 2005. "Menjerat Si Raja Sawit," *Majalah Tempo*, September 12.

Hidayat, Andy Riza. 2007. "Menunggu Pemekaran Tapanuli Selatan?" *Kompas*, April 20.

Hidayat, Syarif. 2009. "*Pilkada*, Money Politics and the Dangers of 'Informal Governance' Practices." In *Deepening Democracy in Indonesia? Direct Elections for Local Leaders (Pilkada)*, edited by Maribeth Erb and Priyambudi Sulistiyanto, 125–146. Singapore: ISEAS.

Honna, Jun. 2009. "From *Dwifungsi* to NKRI: Regime Change and Political Activism of the Indonesian Military." In *Democratization in Post-Suharto Indonesia*, edited by Marco Bunte and Andreas Ufen, 226–247. New York: Routledge.

ICG (International Crisis Group). 2010. *Indonesia: Preventing Violence in Local Elections,* Asia Report No. 197, December 8.

Ini Medan Bung. 2009. "Hj Adlina Milwan Bagi-bagi Duit di Acara HUT Guru," December 7. www.inimedanbung.com.

_____. 2010. "Golkar Labuhanbatu Akan Minta Gubsu Tertibkan PNS Sebagai TS di Pemilukada," January 31. www.inimedanbung.com.

_____. 2011. "HT. Milwan Dilaporkan Ke KPK," February 10. www.inimedanbung .com.

Johan Budi, Agus Riyanto and Bambang Soed. 2000. "Ada Orang Kuat di Torganda?" *Majalah Tempo*, April 3.

Khairul Ikhwan. 2006. "Diterima Wakil Bupati, 1.000 Petani Membubarkan Diri," *Detik.com*, September 21.

Kimura, Ehito. 2010. "Proliferating Provinces: Territorial Politics in Post-Suharto Indonesia." *South East Asia Research* 18.3: 415–449.

Kompas. 2009. "KPU Serdang Bedagai Diperiksa," November 10.

_____. 2009. "Revisi Kawasan Hutan Sumut Masuk Program 100 Hari Menhut," November 18.

_____. 2009. "DK: Pecat KPU Serdang Bedagai," November 27.

_____. 2011. "Satu Tersangka Setiap Pekan," January 18.

KPU Deli Serdang (Komisi Pemilihan Umum Deli Serdang). 2004a. "Berita Acara: Rekapitulasi Hasil Penghitungan Suara Komisi Pemilihan Umum Kabupaten/Kota untuk Pemilihan Umum Anggota DPRD Provinsi," April 21.

_____. 2004b. "Berita Acara Rekapitulasi Hasil Suara Komisi Pemilihan Umum Kabupaten/Kota untuk Pemilihan Umum Anggota DPR dan DPD," April 22.

KPU Labuhanbatu (Komisi Pemilihan Umum Labuhanbatu). 2006. *Laporan: Penyelenggaraan Pemilihan Kepala Daerah & Wakil Kepala Daerah Kabupaten Labuhanbatu Tahun 2005 Buku 1*. Rantauprapat, January.

_____. 2010. "Rekapitulasi Jumlah Pemilih, TPS dan Surat Suara Pemilihan Umum Kepala Daerah dan Wakil Kepala Daerah di Tingkat Kabupaten," Rantauprapat, June 18.

KPU Sergai (Komisi Pemilihan Umum Serdang Bedagai). 2005. "Berita Acara Rekapitulasi Acara Hasil Penghitungan Suara Pemilihan Kepala Daerah dan Wakil Kepala Daerah di Tingkat Kabupaten/Kota oleh Komisi Pemilihan Umum Daerah Kabupaten/Kota," July 2.

_____. 2010. "Daftar Riwayat Hidup (Bio Data) Pasangan Calon Kepala Daerah dan Wakil Kepala Daerah Kabupaten Serdang Bedagai."

KPU Sumut (Komisi Pemilihan Umum Sumatera Utara). 2004. "Data Calon Terpilih Anggota DPRD Sumut Per Daerah Pemilihan." Accessed April 13, 2010, www.kpusumut.org.

_____. 2005. "Rekapitulasi Jumlah Pemilih, PPK PPS, TPS, Dan Hasil Perolehan Suara Masing-Masing Pasangan Calon dalam Pemilihan Kepala Daerah Kabupaten / Kota Tahun 2005 di Provinsi Sumatera Utara (Tahap 1)." Accessed April 13, 2010, www.kpusumut.org.

_____. 2010a. "Daftar Perolehan Suara Calon Kepala Daerah dan Wakil Kepala Daerah Kabupaten Kota Se Sumatera Utara Pemilukada Tanggal 12 Mei 2010."

_____. 2010b. "Daftar Perolehan Suara Calon Kepala Daerah dan Wakil Kepala Daerah Kabupaten Kota Se Sumatera Utara: Pemilukada Tanggal 16 Juni 2010."

KPU Tapsel (Komisi Pemilihan Umum Tapanuli Selatan). 2005a. "Daftar Nama Pasangan Calon Kepala Daerah dan Wakil Kepala Daerah yang Terdaftar di

KPU Kabupaten Tapanuli Selatan," Divisi Peserta Pemilu dan Pencalonan, April 8.

_____. 2005b. "Surat Nomor: 270/ 436 /KPU-TS/V/05, Perihal: Permintaan Klarifikasi Calon Kepala Daerah dan Wakil Kepala Daerah dari DPD Partai Golkar Kabupaten Tapanuli Selatan," May 2.

_____. 2005c. "Berita Acara No: 31/KPU-TS/V/05 Tentang Surat Nomor 270/436/KPU-TS/V/05 tanggal 02 Mei 2005 perihal Permintaan Klarifikasi Calon Kepala Daerah dan Wakil Depala Daerah dari DPD Partai GOLKAR Kabupaten Tapanuli Selatan," May 11.

_____. 2010. "Rincian Perolehan Suara Sah dan Tidak Sah Pemilihan Umum Kepala Daerah dan Wakil Kepala Daerah: Kabupaten Tapanuli Selatan dari Setiap Kecamatan dalam Wilayah Kabupaten."

Kuhonta, Erik, Dan Slater, and Tuong Vu. 2008. "Introduction: The Contributions of Southeast Asian Political Studies." In *Southeast Asia in Political Science: Theory, Region and Qualitative Analysis,* edited by Erik Kuhonta, Dan Slater, and Tuong Vu, 1–29. Stanford: Stanford University Press.

Labuhanbatu News. 2008. "Dugaan Suap Mutasi Ratusan Kasek Dilapor: Polisi Menolak, Jaksa Menerima," August 7. labuhanbatunews.wordpress.com.

_____. 2008. "Kapolres Tunggu Freddy Melapor," October 27. labuhanbatunews. wordpress.com.

Malley, Michael. 1999. "Regions: Centralization and Resistance." In *Indonesia Beyond Suharto: Polity, Economy, Society, Transition,* edited by Donald Emmerson, 71–105. Armonk, NY: M.E. Sharpe.

McCarthy, John. 2002. "Power and Interest on Sumatra's Rainforest Frontier: Clientelist Coalitions, Illegal Logging and Conservation in the Alas Valley." *Journal of Southeast Asian Studies* 33.1: 77–106.

_____. 2007. "Sold down the river: Renegotiating Public Power over Nature in Central Kalimantan." In *Renegotiating Boundaries: Local Politics in Post-Suharto Indonesia,* edited by Henk Schulte Nordholt and Gerry van Klinken. Leiden: KITLV Press: 151–176.

Media Indonesia. 2005. "Konflik Jelang Pesta Rakyat," May 6.

Metro Rantau. 2009. "Ikut Mencalon, Dr Tigor 'Dipecat' dari RSUD," November 12.

_____. 2010. "Cabup Labuhan Batu 'Perang Baliho,'" May 31.

_____. 2010. "Kampanye Terakhir Pasangan HATI di Lapangan Ika Bina: Syamsul Arifin: Dokter Tak Layak jadi Bupati," June 14.

_____. 2010. "Mengawal Jargon Perubahan Pemerintahan ala dr Tigor-Suhari," September 2.

_____. 2010. "Terminal Padang Bulan Resmi Beroperasi," September 3.

_____. 2010. "Bupati Intervensi Kadiskanla Minta Koleganya Dimenangkan," October 1.

_____. 2010. "Orang Dekat Hj Adlina Jadi Tersangka Kasus Calo CPNS," October 14.

Metro Tabagsel. 2010. "Salam 4, Sarasi di Hati Rakyat Tapsel," May 7.

_____. 2010. "Rakyat Siap Menangkan SARASI," May 8.

_____. 2010. "Chairuman: Tapsel harus Maju Pesat," May 9.

_____. 2011. "Dari Rakerda Partai Berlambang Pohon Beringin di Sipirok," February 26.

Mietzner, Marcus. 2006. "Local Democracy: Old Elites Are Still in Power, but Direct Elections Now Give Voters a Chance." *Inside Indonesia* 85 (Jan-Mar): 17–18.

_____. 2009a. "Indonesia and the Pitfalls of Low-Quality Democracy: A Case Study of the Gubernatorial Elections in North Sulawesi." In *Democratization in Post-Suharto Indonesia,* edited by Marco Bunte and Andreas Ufen, 124–150. New York: Routledge.

_____. 2009b. "Political Opinion Polling in Post-Authoritarian Indonesia: Catalyst or Obstacle to Democratic Consolidation?" *Bijdragen tot de Taal-, Land- en Volkenkunde* 165.1: 95–126.

Munthe, Hardi. 2007. "SK Menhut 22/2005 Masih Bermasalah," Walhi Sumatera Utara Press Release No. 07/PR/WSU/V/07, July 20. walhisumut.wordpress.com.

Nasution, Ikhwan. 2010. "Pemindahan Ibukota Tapsel: Rapolo Dinilai Tidak Konsisten," *Medan Bisnis*, October 5.

Ockey, James. 2000. "The Rise of Local Power in Thailand: Provincial Crime, Elections and the Bureaucracy." In *Money and Power in Provincial Thailand,* edited by Ruth McVey, 74–96. Singapore: ISEAS.

Pos Metro Medan. 2010. "Dipukul Oknum Satpol PP Sergai, Wartawan Dituntut 4 Bulan Bui," February 25.

_____. 2011. "Kasasi Terdakwa Korupsi Ditolak, Mantan Sekdakab DS Dibui 2 Tahun," January 14.

Ramidi, Hambali Batubara and Maria Hasugian. 2006. "Setelah Hutan Habis Ditebang," *Majalah Tempo*, September 18.

Reid, Anthony. 1979. *The Blood of the People: Revolution and the End of Traditional Rule in Northern Sumatra.* Kuala Lumpur: Oxford University Press.

Ritonga, S Togi. 2008a. "Wujudkan Pemekaran, Drs Bachrum Harahap Pantas Pimpin Paluta (Bagian I)," *Harian Mandiri*, September 8. harianmandiri.wordpress.com.

_____. 2008b. "Wujudkan Pemekaran, Drs Bachrum Harahap Pantas Pimpin Paluta (Bagian II)," *Harian Mandiri*, September 17. harianmandiri.wordpress.com.

Ryter, Loren. 2009. "Their Moment in the Sun: The New Indonesian Parliamentarians from the Old OKP." In *State of Authority: The State in Society in Indonesia,* edited by Gerry van Klinken and Joshua Barker, 181–218. Ithaca: Cornell SEAP.

Schulte Nordholt, Henk. 2003. "Renegotiating Boundaries: Access, Agency and Identity in Post-Suharto Indonesia," *Bijdragen tot de Taal-, Land- en Volkenkunde* 159: 550–589.

Scott, James. 1972. "Patron-Client Politics and Political Change in Southeast Asia." *American Political Science Review* 66.1: 91–113.

Shefter, Martin. 1994. *Political Parties and the State: The American Historical Experience*. Princeton: Princeton University Press.

Sidel, John. 1999. *Capital, Coercion, and Crime: Bossism in the Philippines*. Stanford: Stanford University Press.

_____. 2004. "Bossism and Democracy in the Philippines, Thailand, and Indonesia: Towards an Alternative Framework for the Study of 'Local Strongmen.'" In *Politicising Democracy: The New Local Politics of Democratisation*, edited by John Harriss, Kristian Stokke, and Olle Törnquist, 51–74. New York: Palgrave Macmillan.

Sinar Indonesia Baru. 2008. "Pendukung Berat Bupati Labuhanbatu Mulai Jaga Jarak," November 4.

_____. 2008. "Pemprovsu Melalui APBD Sumut 2008 Alokasikan Rp 3 Miliar Pada 6 Daerah Tk II," December 17.

_____. 2009. "MPI Labuhanbatu Dilantik, H Ramli Siagian Ketua," April 11.

_____. 2009. "DPRD Labuhanbatu Soroti Belanja Daerah Tak Capai Target, F-PDIP: Anggaran Belanja Daerah Rp64 M Lebih 'Nongkrong' di Bank," August 30.

_____. 2009. "GOR Rantauprapat Terbesar dan Termegah di Sumut Berbiaya Rp 14,95 Kini Mulai Retak," November 20.

_____. 2010. "Ribuan Orang Iringi Pasangan Syahrul M Pasaribu Aldinz Rapolo Siregar Mendaftar ke KPU Tapsel," February 12.

_____. 2010. "Ratusan Warga Unjuk Rsa (sic) Minta KPU Labuhanbatu Benar-benar Verifikasi Berkas Balon Bupati," April 13.

_____. 2010. "Gubsu Apresiasi Bupati 5 Tahun Memimpin, 125 Penghargaan Berhasil Diraih," April 24.

_____. 2010. "Diduga Aniaya Kacab Bank Sumut Panyabungan Oknum, Kepala Bappeda Tapsel Ditangkap Polres Tapsel," May 12.

_____. 2010a. "Ribuan Abang Betor Rantauprapat Ikut Pasang Taruhan Piala Dunia, Uangnya dari Upah Kampanye?" June 14.

_____. 2010b. "Mendagri Harapkan Seluruh Pemda Miliki Unit Kerja Pelayanan Publik Terpadu," June 14.

Slater, Dan. 2004. "Indonesia's Accountability Trap: Party Cartels and Presidential Power after Democratic Transition." *Indonesia* 78: 61–92.

_____. 2010. *Ordering Power: Contentious Politics and Authoritarian Leviathans in Southeast Asia*. Cambridge: Cambridge University Press.

Smith, Claire. 2009. "The Return of the Sultan? Patronage, Power, and Political Machines in 'Post'-Conflict North Maluku." In *Deepening Democracy in Indonesia? Direct Elections for Local Leaders (Pilkada)*, edited by Maribeth Erb and Priyambudi Sulistiyanto, 303–326. Singapore: ISEAS.

Stokes, Susan. 2005. "Perverse Accountability: A Formal Model of Machine Politics with Evidence from Argentia." *American Political Science Review* 99.3 (August): 315–325.

Stoler, Ann. 1985. *Capitalism and Confrontation in Sumatra's Plantation Belt, 1870–1979.* New Haven: Yale University Press.

Suara Karya Online. 2005. "Hasil Pilkada Sergai Tak Bisa Dibatalkan," August 30. www.suarakarya-online.com.

_____. 2005. "Mendagri Diprotes Massa Serdang Bedagai," September 29. www .suarakarya-online.com.

Suara Pembaruan. 2006. "16 Provinsi Usulkan Bagi Hasil Sektor Perkebunan Milik Negara," May 12.

Sukardi Rinakit. 2005. "Indonesian Regional Elections in Praxis." *IDSS Commentaries* No. 65. Singapore: Institute of Defence and Strategic Studies, September 27.

Sumut Pos. 2005. "Buntut Keluarnya SK Nomor 22 Tahun 2005 Soal Perubahan Balon KDH Golkar: KPUD Tapsel Pecah, Ketuanya Sering Diteror," May 18.

_____. 2010. "Chairullah Diperiksa KPK, Johan: Kami Mengusut Kasus Sergai," March 26.

Tomsa, Dirk. 2009. "Uneven Party Institutionalization, Protracted Transition and the Remarkable Resilience of Golkar." In *Democratization in Post-Suharto Indonesia,* edited by Marco Bunte and Andreas Ufen, 176–198. New York: Routledge.

Tilly, Charles. 1978. *From Mobilization to Revolution.* Reading, MA: Addison-Wesley.

Tsai, Yen-ling and Douglas Kammen. 2012. "Anti-Communist Violence and the Ethnic Chinese in Medan, North Sumatra." In *The Contours of Mass Violence in Indonesia, 1965–1968,* edited by Douglas Kammen and Katharine McGregor. Singapore: NUS Press for the Asian Studies Association of Australia.

van Klinken, Gerry. 2009. "Patronage Democracy in Indonesia." In *Rethinking Popular Representation,* edited by Olle Törnquist, Neil Webster, and Kristian Stokke. New York: Palgrave Macmillan.

van Klinken, Gerry and Edward Aspinall. 2011. "Building Relations: Corruption, Competition and Cooperation in the Construction Industry." In *The State and Illegality in Indonesia,* edited by Edward Aspinall and Gerry van Klinken. Leiden: KITLV Press.

Waspada. 2005a. "Mantan Ketua KPUD: Pilkada Tapsel Cacat Hukum," June 29.

_____. 2005b. "Pilkada Binjai Dan Sergai Tak Mulus," June 29.

_____. 2007. "Paripurna Revisi Usulan Pemekaran Tapsel Ricuh, Anggota Dewan Dari PKS Dibogem," April 21.

_____. 2007. "Usulan Pemekaran Tapsel Direvisi," April 24.

_____. 2010. "HT Erry Nuradi Pimpin Partai Golkar Sergai," February 17.

_____. 2010. "Ribuan Massa Hadiri Deklarasi Koalisi Parpol Pendukung Hj Adlina-Trisno," March 23.

Waspada Online. 2007. "Ketua FPG DPRD Tapsel Dituntut 6 Bulan Penjara," September 29. www.waspada.co.id.

_____. 2007. "HT Milwan Dicopot Sebagai Ketua Golkar Labuhan Batu," November 22. www.waspada.co.id.

_____. 2008. "Temuan BPK, Ratusan Juta Dana APBD Labuhan Batu 'Menguap;'" May 28. www.waspada.co.id.

_____. 2009. "Rahudman Harahap tak layak Pj walikota Medan," June 29. www .waspada.co.id.

_____. 2009. "Masyarakat kesalkan pejabat Tidak tinggal di Serdang Bedagai: Pemkab segera bangun Rumah Dinas," July 14. www.waspada.co.id.

_____. 2010. "Poltabes Medan kembali panggil OK David Purba," March 3. www .waspada.co.id.

YIPD (Yayasan Inovasi Pemerintahan Daerah). 2009. "Unit Pelayanan Perijinan Terpadu Satu Pintu, Melawan 'Penyakit Birokrasi,' Meningkatkan Retribusi." *Seri Pendokumentasian Best Practices Inovasi Kabupaten di Indonesia, BKKSI 2008*, February 6. Accessed April 1, 2011, www.yipd.or.id.